LATIN
Grammar

STUDENT TEXT

Second Edition
Revised and Expanded

Douglas Wilson
Karen Craig

Canon Press
MOSCOW, IDAHO

Douglas Wilson and Karen Craig, *Latin Grammar Book I (Student Text)*

First Edition © 1992 by Douglas Wilson
Second Edition © 1997 by Douglas Wilson and Karen Craig

Published 1997 by Canon Press, P.O. Box 8741, Moscow, ID 83843
800-488-2034

Printed in the United States of America

ISBN: 1-885767-37-4

This book is dedicated to Luke,
whose commitment to the education of his children
has been exemplary.

TABLE OF CONTENTS

WHY LATIN?

As with many other valuable things there is difficulty associated with learning Latin. But unlike other subjects, before the process is even begun, there is an additional obstacle to be overcome. That obstacle can be summarized with the simple question—*Why Latin?* For many moderns, the attempt to study this language is nothing more than a quaint irrelevance. What possible reasons can be given for a serious study of Latin? It is a reasonable question. Here are just a few answers:

1. Approximately fifty percent of the vocabulary in our language comes from Latin. This means that students of Latin are not just learning Latin—they are learning to be much more proficient in their own language. It has been shown that verbal scores on standardized tests increase dramatically with the study of Latin. So even when students do not stay with the formal study of Latin after they graduate, it is still a great ongoing benefit to them. The study of Latin grammar is also a great help in understanding the nature of grammar, and that carries over into English as well.

2. The study of Latin provides an understanding of the impact the classical cultures had on our modern culture. We see this in our architecture, the names of planets and constellations, our political structures, Latin expressions that are simply carried over into our language, *et cetera*.

3. Students of Latin are trained in a method of rigorous analysis. The ability that is acquired in doing this is not limited to Latin. So the study of Latin equips young minds to encounter unfamiliar material in a disciplined way. Latin trains the student in the essentials of scientific method: observation, comparison, and generalization.

4. The study of Latin is a great help in developing an appreciation for great literature. Not only may the student be introduced to classical authors like Virgil, he will also be equipped to appreciate English literature much more. This is because many of the great writers in English were steeped in classical literature, and allusions to classical literature and life abound in their writings.

5. Latin provides a wonderful introduction to the study of modern languages. The Romance languages like Spanish, French, Italian, etc. are direct descendants of Latin (unlike English), and the study of Latin is a very appropriate introduction to modern language study.

PRONUNCIATION

REGULARITY

The pronunciation of Latin, unlike English, is very regular. The sounds represented by the letters of the Latin alphabet will never be more than two, while in English the number of sounds for a given letter may be up to five.

In addition, Latin has no silent letters—everything is pronounced. For example, in English the letter *e* on the end of *dare* is not pronounced at all. Furthermore, the word only has one syllable. But in Latin, the same combination of letters would give us two syllables, and the sound *dah re*.

ALPHABET

The Latin alphabet is easy to learn because it is virtually the same as the English alphabet. The only difference is that Latin has no *w*.

In ancient Latin, there was also no *j*, and the sounds of *u* and *v* were represented by one letter. If these are subtracted, we see that classical Latin had twenty-three letters instead of the twenty-six in English. And from these twenty-three, *y* and *z* were seldom used.

THE VOWELS

Latin vowels are the same as English vowels—*a*, *e*, *i*, *o*, and *u*. In Latin, they each have two sounds, long and short. In this book, the long vowels are marked with a *macron* above the vowel. If the vowel is unmarked, then it is short.

LONG	SHORT
a = a in *father*	**a** = a in *idea*
e = e in *obey*	**e** = e in *bet*
i = i in *machine*	**i** = i in *this*
o = o in *holy*	**o** = o in *domain*
u = u in *rude*	**u** = u in *put*

In the phonetic exercises, spell out the various vowel sounds this way:

A long *a* should be *ah*, as in *blah*.
A long *e* should be *ay*, as in *day*.
A long *i* should be *ee*, as in *see*.
A long *o* should be *oh*, as in *oh*.
A long *u* should be *oo*, as in *zoo*.

The short vowels can be represented in those exercises simply with their respective letters. The common endings *us* and *um* should be represented by *us* and *um* respectively.

DIPTHONGS

A dipthong is a blending of two vowels in order to form a single sound. The most important for you to learn will be *ae*, *au*, and *oe*. Their pronunciation is as follows:

ae = This sounds like the *ai* in *aisle* or like the *i* in *like*.
The Latin word *caelum* would therefore sound like *keye lum*.

au = This sounds like the *ou* in *bound*.
The Latin word *aut* would sound like the English *out*.

oe = This sounds like the *oi* in *soil*.
The Latin word *coepit* is therefore pronounced *coy pit*.

Note: In words like *poēta,* the *ē* has its own syllable and is not part of the dipthong. There are three other dipthongs which are not as important. They are *ei*, which should be pronounced like the *ei* in *vein*; *eu*, which should be pronounced like the *eu* in *feud*; and *ui*, which sounds like the *ui* in *ruin*.

Consonants

Generally the consonants will sound as they do in English. The consonants that sound just the same are as follows:

B, D, F, H, K, L, M, N, P, Z

You should also realize that the exceptions are the result of the *regularity* of Latin, and so they should not be hard to remember. Below is a list of the exceptions.

C and **ch** sound like *k*.
The word *centum* is pronounced *ken tum*.
The word *pulcher* is pronounced *pul ker*.

G has a hard sound, as in *go*.
The word *regio* is pronounced *re gi oh*.

J (if you ever see a *j* from more recent Latin) is like the *y* in *yes*.
So *jūdex* is pronounced *yoo dex*.

S has only the sound heard in *sill*.

T has only the sound heard in *ton*. It does *not* combine with *i* as it does in English to make a *sh* sound—as in *ration*.

V in Latin makes the sound of our *w*.
Vocō is pronounced this way—*wo koh*

X has only the sound of a *ks* and is pronounced with the preceding vowel.
Exemplar is pronounced *eks em plar*.

Bs and **bt** are the same as *ps* and *pt*.
Urbs is pronounced *urps*.

Ph and **th** have an almost invisible *h*, so that they sound like *p* and *t*.
Pantheon is pronounced *Pan te on*.

SYLLABLES

In Latin, a syllable must always contain a vowel or a dipthong. Here are two basic rules for division of syllables.

If there is a consonant between two vowels, the consonant is pronounced with the vowel that *follows* it. For example, *habeō* is divided this way—*ha be ō*.

If there are two consonants between two vowels, then the first consonant goes with the vowel that preceeds, and the second goes with the vowel that follows. For example, *terra* is divided this way—*ter ra*.

ACCENT

In English, learning how to accent a word is a matter of sheer memory. But in Latin the accent falls according to definite and set patterns. Here are three basic rules.

1. All words of two syllables are accented on the first syllable. For example, *A mō* and *POR tant*.

2. In a word of more than two syllables, if the next to last syllable contains a long vowel or dipthong, for example, *lau DA mus,* or if its vowel is followed by two consonants, then the accent falls on that syllable, for example, *im POR tant.*

3. In a word of more than two syllables, if the next to last syllable contains a short vowel, and it is followed by only one consonant, or another vowel, then the accent falls on the third from the last syllable. For example, *e PIS tu la.*

EXERCISE ONE

A. The purpose of this exercise is pronunciation only. Next to each word, phonetically spell out how each word sounds in English. Do not be concerned with the meanings of the words.

1. agricolam   *ah gri koh lum*
2. poētae   *poh ay teye*
3. fēminās   *fay mi nahs*
4. dōnum   *doh num*
5. dabant   *dah bahnt*
6. dabāmus
7. videō
8. vidēmus
9. habent
10. rem
11. diēs
12. diēbus

13. laudant
14. manibus
15. īnsulārum
16. gaudium
17. nāvigāvit
18. amīcus
19. vulnerō

BASIC GRAMMAR

THE IMPORTANCE OF KNOWING PARTS OF SPEECH

When a student begins the study of a new language, he usually does not have the luxury of learning it the same way he learned his native language. When he was little he learned the basic rules of his own tongue "by ear." Only later, when he was already fluent was he instructed in the formal rules of his language.

But it is different with a new language. Some things can still be learned by ear, but this is not the most efficient way to learn a second language. At some point, it is a great advantage to learn the rules of grammar.

The basic parts of speech listed in this lesson are found in both English and Latin. Their appearance, of course, is different, but the role they play in establishing the meaning of a sentence is the same. Learning (or reviewing) these parts of speech will therefore be an advantage in both languages.

This is provided as a reference for later work. It is *not* intended as a thorough study of grammar, but is assuming that the student has already had basic grammatical instruction.

NOUNS

A *noun* is a word which refers to a *person*, a *place*, or a *thing*. Consequently, words like *dog*, *cat*, *house*, and so forth are all nouns. Words which refer to *abstract things* like *truth*, *love* and *beauty* are also nouns.

VERBS

A *verb* is a word which shows *action*. Thus, when we say *The preacher speaks* the word *speaks* is the verb. It shows the action.

Some verbs also show *existence* or *remaining in a place* instead of action. A sentence like *He is in the Navy now* is a sentence like this. The verb here is *is*. *We shall remain in town* is another. The verb here is *shall remain*.

ADJECTIVES

An adjective is a word which describes a noun. If we were to say *The tall preacher speaks*, the adjective here is the word *tall* because it describes a noun—*preacher*.

Sometimes an adjective will describe a noun which is not there, but is understood by implication anyway. We see this in the cliche *The good die young*. The word *good* is an adjective, even though the noun it describes (people) is absent from the sentence. We also see this in the words of our Lord—*the meek shall inherit the earth.*

ADVERBS

An adverb is a word which describes a verb. When we say *The tall preacher speaks powerfully* the word *powerfully* helps to describe the verb, which is *speaks*.

PRONOUNS

A pronoun is a word which is used in the place of a noun. In the sentence *The woman saw the general and greeted him* the pronoun *him* is used instead of using the noun *general* a second time.

The word that is replaced by the pronoun is called the *antecedent* of the pronoun. In the sentence above the antecedent of *him* is *general*.

TYPES OF PRONOUNS

Some pronouns are called PERSONAL PRONOUNS. They are the pronouns *I, me, you, he, him, she, her, it, we, us, they,* and *them.*

Another type of pronoun is called the INTERROGATIVE PRONOUN. They are used to enable us to ask questions—*who, which,* and *what?*

And when these same pronouns are used in sentences which are not questions, we call them RELATIVE PRONOUNS. Consider the following:

> *The preacher who spoke powerfully was my uncle.*

In this sentence, the word *who* is being used as a relative pronoun. In some sentences the word *that* is also used as a relative pronoun. For example:

> *The woman that just entered the room is my mother.*

There are also DEMONSTRATIVE PRONOUNS. They are the pronouns *this, these, that, those.* They are used to point out, or to show (to demonstrate!) a specific object which has been previously mentioned. Study the example:

> *Did he touch this yellow apple or that (one)?*

In this sentence, *that* is being used as a demonstrative pronoun. It points out which apple the boy may have touched.

EXERCISE TWO

A. Please answer the following questions about parts of speech.

1. What is a noun?

2. Give three examples of English nouns.

3. What is a verb?

4. Give three examples of English verbs.

5. What is an adjective?

6. Give three examples of English adjectives.

7. Give an example of an adjective replacing a noun

8. What is an adverb?

9. Give three examples of English adverbs.

10. What is a personal pronoun?

11. Give three examples of English personal pronouns.

VERBS

In Latin, the function of a verb in a sentence is determined by the ending of the verb. That ending varies according to three basic variables. They are, respectively, *tense*, *person*, and *number*.

TENSE

You should recall that a verb displays action. Now the tense of a verb indicates *when* that action occurs. In this book we will be concerned with *six tenses*. They are:

PRESENT TENSE shows action *right now*.
> Iulia *laudat* Deum.
> Julia *praises* God.

IMPERFECT TENSE shows *continuous* action *in the past*.
> Iulia *laudābat* Deum.
> Julia *was praising* God.

FUTURE TENSE shows action that *will* happen *in the future*.
> Iulia *laudābit* Deum.
> Julia *will praise* God.

PERFECT TENSE shows *completed* action *in the past*.
> Iulia *laudāvit* Deum.
> Julia *praised* God.

PLUPERFECT TENSE shows *completed* action *prior to* some time in the past.
> Iulia *laudāverat* Deum.
> Julia *had praised* God.

FUTURE PERFECT TENSE shows completed action prior to some point in the future.
> Iulia *laudāverit* Deum.
> Julia *will have praised* God.

PERSON AND NUMBER

Within each tense, there are six possible endings for each verb. This can be seen most easily if we arrange each tense of each verb in two columns of three lines each. The first column is *singular* (which refers to *one*), and the second is *plural* (which refers to more than *one*). Elsewhere in this book *singular* will be abbreviated as *sing.* and *plural* as *pl*.

Each of the three lines represents what is called the *person*—the first line is called *first person*, the second *second person*, and the third is *third person*. This gives us six different possible combinations.

First person refers to *I* and *we*. Second person refers to *you* and *you all*. Third person refers to *he*, *she*, *it*, and *they*.

For example: This is the verb *praise* conjugated in English in the present tense.

	SINGULAR	PLURAL
FIRST PERSON	(I) praise	(we) praise
SECOND PERSON	(you) praise	(you) praise
THIRD PERSON	(he, she, or it) praises	(they) praise

In Latin, the same verb looks like this:

	SINGULAR	PLURAL
FIRST PERSON	laudō	laudāmus
SECOND PERSON	laudās	laudātis
THIRD PERSON	laudat	laudant

You should notice right away that the conjugation of a verb in Latin is much more regular and orderly than it is in English. This is because the pronoun is implied in the verb.

HOW MANY ENDINGS?

Because we will be learning six different tenses, and each tense has six different endings for the verb, this means that for each verb the student will be learning thirty-six different endings. The endings will be learned separately.

FIRST CONJUGATION VERBS

We come now to the first family of verbs, called the First Conjugation. We will begin our study of the First Conjugation by looking at it in the present tense.

As was mentioned before, the present tense of a verb represents action *right now*. In English, there are three different ways to say this, while in Latin there is only one. For example, if we were to use the verb *praise* in the present tense in English, we could say any one of the following three sentences:

1. *I praise.*   This is a simple "declarative" statement. It states the action.
2. *I am praising.*   This is a "progressive" statement. The actions is in process.
3. *I do praise.*   This is an "emphatic" statement. The action is emphasized.

But in Latin, there is only one way to say this—*laudō*. So let's walk through the present tense for the First Conjugation. We will use *laudō* for our sample.

	SINGULAR	PLURAL
FIRST PERSON	*laudō*—I praise	*laudāmus*—we praise
SECOND PERSON	*laudās*—you praise	*laudātis*—you praise
THIRD PERSON	*laudat*—he, she, or it praises	*laudant*—they praise

The conjugational endings of the present tense can be memorized this way—*ō, s, t! mus, tis, nt!* In most cases, these endings are placed on the stem of the verb (*laudā*) to form the various combinations. The only place the entire stem is not seen is in the first person singular—because the stem ends with an *a*, and because it is hard to pronounce the *ō* following, the *aō* collapsed into an *ō*. Thus, *laudaō* became simply *laudō*.

DICTIONARY

When you look up a verb, you will look it up in its singular form for the first person. For this verb, you would look up *laudō*. A verb is listed in the following way:

> *laudō, -āre, -āvī, -ātum*—praise

This is a shorthand way of representing this:

> *laudō, laudāre, laudāvī, laudātum*—praise

These are called the FOUR PRINCIPAL PARTS of a verb. When you learn a new verb, it is important that you learn these four forms. If you do not, then you will be unable to recognize some forms of verbs which you really know. And if you learn these Four Principal Parts, then you will be able to build from them any form of any verb.

The First Principal Part is called the verb's PRESENT ACTIVE TENSE. The Second Principal Part is the PRESENT ACTIVE INFINITIVE. The second form here (*laudāre*) is the infinitive of the verb. The infinitive of the verb *laudāre* is rendered in English as *to praise*. The stem is found by dropping the *-re* from the end. This gives you *laudā*—the stem. This is the part of the verb you will use to build various forms you will need for the Present System (present, imperfect, and future tenses) and the imperative. The uses for the Third and Fourth Principal Parts will be covered in subsequent chapters.

COMMANDS

The Second Principal Part (the infinitive) helps us in several ways. If the *-re* is dropped from the infinitive, we have already learned that it shows us the stem of the verb. For example, if we drop the *-re* from *laudāre* we have the stem *laudā*. We then attach the endings for the present, imperfect or future tense, depending on what we want to say.

But *laudā* by itself is a command to one person. It is the command to praise. Therefore, we say that *laudā* is the singular imperative of the verb *laudō*. And if we replace the *-re* with a *-te* it is a command to more than one person to praise—*laudāte!*

VOCABULARY

[NOTE: In the first several lessons of this book, the vocabulary lists are quite long. If you have used Canon Press's Latin Primer III, most of these words are review. If you are new to Latin study, divide the lists and memorize 5-10 words each day. You will need to refer to the list for your exercises, but frequent use is also a good way to learn vocabulary!]

All the verbs in this list are First Conjugation verbs. They are listed with their Four Principal Parts.

accusō, -āre, -āvī, -ātum	to accuse, to blame
agitō, -āre, -āvī, -ātum	to drive, to arouse, to disturb
amō, -āre, -āvī, -ātum	to love
appropinquō, -āre, -āvī, -ātum	to approach, to draw near to
clamō, -āre, -āvī, -ātum	to shout
conciliō, -āre, -āvī, -ātum	to win over
conservō, -āre, -āvī, -ātum	to save, to preserve
convocō, -āre, -āvī, -ātum	to call together
damnō, -āre, -āvī, -ātum	to condemn
dēmōnstrō, -āre, -āvī, -ātum	to point out, to show
*dō, dare, dedī, datum	to give
errō, -āre, -āvī, -ātum	to err, to wander, to be mistaken
explorō, -āre, -āvī, -ātum	to explore
habitō, -āre, -āvī, -ātum	to dwell, to live in, to inhabit
laborō, -āre, -āvī, -ātum	to labor
laudō, -āre, -āvī, -ātum	to praise
mandō, -āre, -āvī, -ātum	to entrust
mutō, -āre, -āvī, -ātum	to change, to alter
narrō, -āre, -āvī, -ātum	to tell
navigō, -āre, -āvī, -ātum	to sail
oppugnō, -āre, -āvī, -ātum	to attack
portō, -āre, -āvī, -ātum	to carry
postulō, -āre, -āvī, -ātum	to demand
pugnō, -āre, -āvī, -ātum	to fight
rogō, -āre, -āvī, -ātum	to ask
spectō, -āre, -āvī, -ātum	to look at, to watch
*stō, stāre, stetī, statum	to stand
tardō, -āre, -āvī, -ātum	to slow down, to delay
vexō, -āre, -āvī, -ātum	to harass, to vex, to annoy, to ravage
vocō, -āre, -āvī, -ātum	to call
vulnerō, -āre, -āvī, -ātum	to wound

*Dō and stō have Third Principal parts which do not follow the -āre, -āvī, -ātum pattern. Memorize their four principal parts. Dō also does not have macrons in its stem except in first and second person present tense. Like this: dō, dās, dat, damus, datis, dant.

In order to conjugate these verbs in the present tense, simply attach the endings (ō, s, t, mus, tis, nt) to the stem. Thus, for example:

vocō, vocās, vocat, vocāmus, vocātis, vocant
amō, amās, amat, amāmus, amātis, amant

These verbs of the First Conjugation all have something in common—which is why they are grouped together in the First Conjugation. You should notice that they all have the letter -*ā* at the end of their stem. This is the characteristic feature of the First Conjugation.

Exercise Three

A. Spell out in English how each Latin word should be pronounced and place the accent properly.

1. laudō

2. laudās

3. laudat

4. laudāmus

5. laudātis

6. laudant

B. Chant the following paradigms ten times through.

ō, s, t! mus, tis, nt!
amō, amās, amat! amāmus, amātis, amant!

C. Translate the following English into Latin.

1. You (singular) praise.

2. We preserve.

3. She explores.

4. He shouts.

5. They love.

6. You (plural) praise.

7. I delay.

D. Translate the following Latin into English.

1. Laudāmus.

2. Oppugnant.

3. Stātis.

4. Portās.

5. Narrō.

6. Navigat.

7. Spectā!

8. Amāte!

9. Portāte!

10. Dā!

E. List all the English words you can think of which come from this lesson's vocabulary words.

1.	11.
2.	12.
3.	13.
4.	14.
5.	15.
6.	16.
7.	17.
8.	18.
9.	19.
10.	20.

F. Answer the following questions.

1. What is a dipthong?

2. In Latin, what sound does *ae* make?

3. In Latin, what sound does *v* make?

4. In words of two syllables, where does the accent fall?

5. What is a noun?

6. What is a verb?

7. List the six tenses we will study in this book.

8. To what time does the pluperfect tense refer?

9. The pronoun *they* is associated with what person, and what number?

10. How many endings are there for each tense?

11. What is the first person singular ending for First Conjugation verbs?

12. What is the third person plural ending for First Conjugation verbs?

13. What is the characteristic feature of First Conjugation verbs?

14. How is the stem of First Conjugation verbs found?

15. When a verb is looked up in a dictionary, how many forms of the verb will be seen?

NOUNS

CASES

This is an important area where there is a marked difference between English and Latin. In English, we determine what function a noun has in a sentence by *word order*. This is not the case in Latin. For example, if we said:

> *The boy sat on the pew.*

This has a completely different meaning than if we said:

> *The pew sat on the boy.*

In other words, even though we have the same words, and they appear in the same way, we have a completely different meaning—determined by the order of the words.

In Latin, the order of words does not have the same grammatical function. There are certain patterns of word order in Latin—verbs commonly come at the end of the sentence, for example. And there are some situations where word order makes some grammatical difference, but the principal grammatical distinctions are made according to a different system.

Take, for example, the Latin sentence meaning *God loves the world*. It looks like this:

> *Deus mundum amat.*

If we change the word order, the meaning stays the same.

> *Mundum Deus amat.*

This still means *God loves the world*. Now if we want to change the meaning of the sentence, we must change the endings of the nouns. Let us say that we want to reverse the subject and direct object in the sentence—we want to say *The world loves God*. The sentence would become:

> *Mundus Deum amat.*

Notice that we now have *Deum* instead of *Deus*, and *mundus* instead of *mundum*. These different endings are called case endings. There are five different case endings, and they come in both singular and plural for a total of ten endings for each noun. The case endings serve these functions:

NOMINATIVE is the case used when the noun is the *subject* of the sentence.
GENITIVE is the case used to indicate *possession*.
DATIVE is the case used for the *indirect object*.
ACCUSATIVE is the case used for the *direct object*.
ABLATIVE is a case with many functions, but among them is the use of showing manner or means.

DECLENSIONS

There are five basic families of Latin nouns. These families are called declensions. Thus we have the *First Declension*, *Second Declension*, and so forth.

These declensions are distinguished from one another by their distinctive endings. When a noun is learned, you will also learn what declension it is in. (For example, the nouns in the examples above, *Deus* and *mundus*, are from the *Second Declension* which we will learn a little later.) This means that you will only attach the case endings from that declension to that noun. In other words, any given noun belongs to only one family—one declension. It will therefore *only* appear with the ten endings of that declension.

First Declension Nouns

You should remember that the case endings for the First Declension are:

	Singular	Plural
Nominative	vill*a*	vill*ae*
Genitive	vill*ae*	vill*ārum*
Dative	vill*ae*	vill*īs*
Accusative	vill*am*	vill*ās*
Ablative	vill*ā*	vill*īs*

When you memorize these case endings (which you will do), you should go down the singular column, and then down the plural—*a, ae, ae, am, ā! ae, ārum, īs, ās, īs!*

Many of you will have noticed that some of these different case endings are not different at all. For example, the genitive singular and the nominative plural are the same. If the function of a word in a sentence is determined by the ending, then how can this determination be made if the ending is the same? How can you tell them apart? The answer is that when the case endings are the same, you should be able to tell which it is by the context of the sentence.

Dictionary

When you look up a noun in a Latin dictionary, it is important for you to learn the meaning of the word, and the declension of that word. The way this is done is this: the word is listed in its nominative singular form, and is immediately followed by the genitive singular ending. If you have learned the case endings for the declensions, then you will immediately know what declension the word is in.

For example, suppose you look up the word for *girl* in Latin, which is *puella*. When you look it up in the dictionary it will be listed this way:

> *puella*, *-ae*, f., girl

Puella is the nominative singular, and *puellae* is the genitive singular. In other words, they have given you the first two endings, expecting you to be able to finish the remaining eight endings.

The *f.* that follows the genitive singular ending tells us the gender of the noun. In this case, the gender is feminine, represented here with an *f*. If the gender were masculine, then there would be an *m*, and if neuter, an *n*.

Nouns and Verbs

Now let's bring together First Declension nouns and First Conjugation verbs. Just to keep things simple at first, we will limit ourselves to two cases—the nominative and the accusative. You should remember that the *nominative* is the case used when a noun is the *subject* of a sentence and the *accusative* is the case used when a noun is the *direct object*.

Agricolam laudāmus—We praise the farmer.

The *-am* on the end of our noun tells us it is *accusative singular*. This means there is only one farmer, and he is the direct object of the verb. The *-mus* on the end of our verb tells us that the verb is in the *present tense*, and that it is *first person plural*. Therefore the verb means we praise. This is easy, right? Just like English, only different!

 Agricola laudat—The farmer praises.

The procedure is the same here. The *-a* on the end of the noun tells us it is *nominative singular*, making it the subject of the sentence. The *-at* on the end of the verb tells us that a he, she, or it is doing the praising. Because we have a he, she or an it in the nominative case, we conclude that the farmer is the one praising.

But remember, in Latin a verb can stand alone as a complete sentence. This is because every verb contains its own pronoun. If there is no other noun or pronoun in the sentence which fits with the verb, the verb can stand alone. For example, the one word *laudat* means *he praises*.

Verb First!

When you are translating a Latin sentence, always look for the verb *first*. If the verb is in the first person, whether singular or plural, you already have the subject of the sentence (*I* or *we*). If it is second person, singular or plural, you have the subject also (*you*, singular or plural). If it is in the third person, singular or plural, you need to look through the rest of the sentence for nouns in the nominative case.

For example, suppose my verb is:

 vocat—he, she, or it calls.

Before I translate it using the pronoun, I should look over the rest of the sentence to see if there is a noun in the nominative singular. Sure enough, here it is:

 Fēmina vocat.—The woman calls.

Varying the Tense

The tense of the verb will not affect the endings of the nouns. For example, we may want to say:

 Puellam vocat.—He calls the girl.
 Puellam vocābat.—He was calling the girl.
 Puellam vocābit.—He will call the girl.

In each one of these sentences, the tense of the verb is different, but the noun *puellam* remains in the accusative case.

Gender

First Declension nouns are almost always feminine. There are only four commonly used nouns of the First Declension which are masculine. They are: *Poēta, Agricola, Incola, and Nauta.* The reason the gender of a noun is important is because adjectives in Latin must always match the nouns they modify in gender, number, and case—but there will be more on this later.

VOCABULARY

The words in this list are all <u>First Declension Nouns</u>.

agricola, -ae, **m.**	farmer
audacia, -ae, f.	boldness
avāritia, -ae, f.	greed
benevolentia, -ae, f.	favor, good will
coma, -ae, f.	hair, leaves of a tree, foliage
constantia, -ae, f.	constancy, steadfastness
cōpia, -ae, f.	supply, (pl.) troops
culpa, -ae, f.	fault, blame, sin
cūra, -ae, f.	care, worry
dīvitiae, -ārum, f.	wealth, riches
fābula, -ae, f.	story, legend
fāma, -ae, f.	rumor, report
famula, -ae, f.	maidservant, female slave
fēmina, -ae, f.	woman
fenestra, -ae, f.	window
flamma, -ae, f.	flame
harēna, -ae, f.	sand, beach
hōra, -ae, f.	hour
incola, -ae, **m.**	inhabitant, settler, colonist
īnsula, -ae, f.	island
latebra, -ae, f.	hiding place, lair, hideout
littera, -ae, f.	letter of the alphabet
litterae, -ārum, f.	letter (correspondence)
mensa, -ae, f.	table
mēta, -ae, f.	goal, turning point, limit
misericordia, -ae, f.	pity, mercy
mola, -ae, f.	millstone
nauta, -ae, **m.**	sailor
patella, -ae, f.	small pan or dish
pecūnia, -ae, f.	prize, reward
poena, -ae, f.	penalty, punishment
poēta, -ae, **m.**	poet
prōvincia, -ae, f.	province
puella, -ae, f.	girl
rota, -ae, f.	wheel
sententia, -ae, f.	opinion, decision
silva, -ae, f.	forest
tenebrae, -ārum, f.	gloomy place, darkness, shadows
turba, -ae, f.	crowd, throng, mob
via, -ae, f.	road, way
villa, -ae, f.	villa, farmhouse
vīta, -ae, f.	life

SECOND DECLENSION NOUNS (MASCULINE)

You should remember that the case endings for the Second Declension Masculine Nouns are:

	SINGULAR	PLURAL
NOMINATIVE	Deus	Deī
GENITIVE	Deī	Deōrum
DATIVE	Deō	Deīs
ACCUSATIVE	Deum	Deōs
ABLATIVE	Deō	Deīs

VOCABULARY

All of the nouns in this vocabulary list belong to the *Second Declension Masculine*. Notice how the genitive singular ending is listed after each word, telling you which declension the word is in.

anulus, -ī, m.	ring
campus, -ī, m.	plain, athletic field, level area
capillus, -ī, m.	hair
carrus, -ī, m.	a two-wheeled wagon
cibus, -ī, m.	food
Deus, -ī, m.	God
digitus, -ī, m.	finger, inch
discipulus, -ī, m.	student
dominus, -ī, m.	master, lord
equus, -ī, m.	horse
famulus, -ī, m.	male houseservant, male slave
fīlius, -ī, m.	son
fluvius, -ī, m.	river
fūmus, -ī, m.	smoke
gladius, -ī, m.	sword
hortus, -ī, m.	garden
humus, -ī, m.	ground, earth, land
laurus, -ī, m.	laurel tree
līberī, -ōrum, m.	children
locus, -ī, m.	place
lūcus, -ī, m.	grove
lūdus, -ī, m.	game, play, school
nūntius, ī, m.	messenger
populus, -ī, m.	people
scopulus, -ī, m.	cliff, crag, rock formation
servus, -ī, m.	slave
socius, -ī, m.	ally, companion, associate
tumulus, -ī, m.	mound, hill, burial mound
ventus, -ī, m.	wind

GENDER

There are no feminine nouns of the Second Declension. This leaves us with masculine and neuter. All the Second Declension nouns listed above are masculine. Those nouns which are neuter in the Second Declension are easy to identify because of their modified endings. They are close enough to the masculine endings to be considered part of the same declension, but are distinctive enough to be remembered separately. Here are the *Second Declension Neuter* endings.

SECOND DECLENSION NOUNS (NEUTER)

You should remember that the case endings for the Second Declension Neuter Nouns are:

	SINGULAR	PLURAL
NOMINATIVE	dōn*um*	dōn*a*
GENITIVE	dōn*ī*	dōn*ōrum*
DATIVE	dōn*ō*	dōn*īs*
ACCUSATIVE	dōn*um*	dōn*a*
ABLATIVE	dōn*ō*	dōn*īs*

These endings differ from the masculine endings in just three places. In the nominative singular there is an *-um* in place of an *-us*, and in the plural *-a* replaces both *-ī* and *-ōs*. A characteristic feature of the neuter is also seen here—the nominative and accusative have same endings in both the singular and plural columns.

VOCABULARY

All the nouns below belong to the *Second Declension Neuter*.

aedificium, -ī, n.	building
antrum, -ī, n.	cave
argentum, -ī, n.	silver, money
astrum, -ī, n.	star, constellation
auxilium, -ī, n.	help; (pl.) auxiliary troops
bracchium, bracchī, n.	arm
cōnsilium, -ī, n.	advice, plan
dōnum, -ī, n.	gift
exemplum, -ī, n.	example
fātum, -ī, n.	fate
gaudium, -ī, n.	joy, happiness
lignum, -ī, n.	wood, timber, firewood
perīculum, -ī, n.	danger
praemium, -ī, n.	reward
proelium, -ī, n.	battle
tectum, -ī, n.	roof, building, dwelling
testimōnium, -ī, n.	testimony
vallum, -ī, n.	rampart, wall
vestīgium, vestīgī, n.	footprint, trace, track
vīnum, -ī, n.	wine

FOUR THINGS TO KNOW

Putting all these factors together, there are four important questions you should be able to answer concerning any noun you encounter.

The first is: *To what declension does it belong?* First, second, third, fourth, or fifth?

The second is: *In what case is it?* Nominative, genitive, dative, accusative, or ablative?

The third is: *What number is it?* Singular or plural?

And last: *What gender is it?* Masculine, feminine, or neuter?

Now don't panic! Initially, this may seem very complicated. But if you take each step, one at a time, you will find that it all comes together very naturally.

NOUNS AND VERBS

Now let's put some of the First Conjugation verbs we have learned together with these Second Declension nouns. We will limit ourselves still to two cases—the nominative and the accusative.

> *Deum laudātis*—You (pl.) praise God.
> *Deum laudābimus*—We will praise God.

You should recall that with the verbs used in the two sentences above, the subject of each sentence is contained within the verb. This is because they are in the 1st person and 2nd person, respectively. But consider how it works when the 3rd person is used.

> *Servus Deum laudat*—The slave praises God.

Now if the subject *servus* were not in this sentence, it would still be a complete sentence—*He praises God*. But because we looked at the verb first, saw it was in the 3rd person singular, we could then look through the rest of the sentence to see if there was any noun in the nominative singular to be found. Sure enough, there it was—*servus*.

Now let's put some Second Declension, Neuter nouns together with some verbs and see if we encounter any problems.

> *Dōnum portat.*

Now what do you do first? You look for the verb—which in this case is *portat*. This means *he, she, or it carries*. Because it is a verb in the 3rd person, singular, you look for a noun in the nominative singular. Do you have one? Well, maybe. *Dōnum* could be nominative singular *or* accusative singular. How does one decide? As was discussed earlier, in this kind of situation, the context determines the translation. In other words, translate it both ways, and decide which makes better sense.

> 1. *He carries the gift.*
> 2. *The gift carries.*

Grammatically, either translation is correct. The only problem with the second one is that it does not make any sense. So go with the first translation.

Vocabulary

There are a few extra words which you will soon be needing which are not nouns or verbs. The first four are adverbs, and the last two are conjunctions. As such, these words do not change their endings at all. They will always look like this:

saepe	often
nōn	not
semper	always
cūr	why
et	and
sed	but

EXERCISE FOUR

A. Spell out in English how each Latin word should be pronounced and place the accent properly.

1. mundus

2. mundum

3. Deus

4. amat

5. puella

6. puellam

7. Deum

8. amāmus

9. puellās

10. laudātis

B. Chant each of the following paradigms ten times through.

ō, s, t! mus, tis, nt!
amō, amās, amat! amāmus, amātis, amant!
a, ae, ae, am, ā! ae, ārum, īs, ās, īs!
us, ī, ō, um, ō! ī, ōrum, īs, ōs, īs!
um, ī, ō, um, ō! a, ōrum, īs, a, īs!

C. Translate the following English into Latin.

1. The women praise God, but the poet does not love God.

2. The manservant is giving an example.

3. He looks at the flame, but he does not condemn the son.

4. Greed lives in the settler.

5. The messenger often calls the mob together.

6. The girls are wandering and they approach the forest.

7. Rumor always disturbs the farmer.

8. The sailors explore the island.

9. The cart does carry the women and the maidservants.

10. We are praising God.

D. Translate the following Latin into English.

1. Praemium copiās tardat.

2. Agricolae nautās pugnant.

3. Nautae prōvinciam explorant.

4. Puella Deum appropinquat.

5. Incola silvam habitat.

6. Servī saepe dominōs nōn pugnant.

7. Vestigia periculum dēmōnstrant.

8. Argentum fīlium conciliat.

9. Discipulus dominum spectat.

10. Fēmina comam conservat.

E. List all the English words you can think of which come from the vocabulary learned thus far.

    1.   6.

    2.   7.

    3.   8.

    4.   9.

    5.   10.

F. Answer the following questions.

    1. How many cases are there for Latin nouns?

    2. To what time does the pluperfect tense refer?

    3. How is a *v* pronounced?

    4. What are the suffixes on the end of Latin nouns called?

    5. What is the accusative plural ending for the First Declension?

    6. Does word order determine grammatical function in Latin?

    7. What is the genitive singular ending for the First Declension?

    8. How many cases are there for each noun?

    9. What are the names of these cases?

    10. How many genders are there for Latin nouns?

First Conjugation Imperfect and Future

Imperfect

We are still working with the family of First Conjugations, only now we will be looking at the imperfect and future tenses. Because of this, we will be building off the same stem. As before, we will be using *laudō* for our example.

The imperfect endings are:

bam, bās, bat! bāmus, bātis, bant!

The imperfect tense may be translated *was praising,* or *used to praise.*

You should remember that the stem for *laudō* is *laudā.* We therefore will conjugate this verb in the imperfect tense this way:

	Singular	Plural
First Person	*laudābam*—I was praising	*laudābāmus*—we were praising
Second Person	*laudābās*—you were praising	*laudābātis*—you were praising
Third Person	*laudābat*—he, she, or it was praising	*laudābant*—they were praising

Future

In the First Conjugation, the endings for the future tense are:

bō, bis, bit! bimus, bitis, bunt!

When they are attached to the stem of the verb *laudō,* it looks like this:

	Singular	Plural
First Person	*laudābō*—I will praise	*laudābimus*—we will praise
Second Person	*laudābis*—you will praise	*laudābitis*—you will praise
Third Person	*laudābit*—he, she, or it will praise	*laudābunt*—they will praise

Exercise Five–a

A. Spell out in English how each Latin word should be pronounced and place the accent properly.

1. laudābāmus
2. laudābant
3. vocābant
4. vocant
5. amābāmus
6. amābimus
7. laudābunt
8. spectābunt
9. spectō
10. vocābit

B. Chant each of the following paradigms ten times through.

ō, s, t! mus, tis, nt!

amō, amās, amat! amāmus, amātis, amant!

a, ae, ae, am, ā! ae, ārum, īs, ās, īs!

us, ī, ō, um, ō! ī, ōrum, īs, ōs, īs!

um, ī, ō, um, ō! a, ōrum, īs, a, īs!

bam, bās, bat! bāmus, bātis, bant!

bō, bis, bit! bimus, bitis, bunt!

C. Translate the following review sentences.

1. Deus mundum amat.

2. Puellam amat.

3. Puella amat.

4. Spectāmus.

5. Amātis.

6. Vocant.

7. Vocant puellam.

8. Puella vocat.

9. Puella Deum appropinquat.

10. Vocō.

D. Translate the following English into Latin.

1. They were praising and loving God.

2. I shall always praise God.

3. God was watching the world.

4. The girl and the maid were often praising God.

5. The master will call.

6. The girls will wander.

7. They were shouting the reports.

8. The woman was not carrying the dish.

9. You (pl.) were sailing.

10. You (sing.) will not wound the son.

E. Translate the following Latin into English.
1. Laudābimus.

2. Puellam rogābunt.

3. Puella mutābit.

4. Deus amābat.

5. Deum amābat.

6. Famulī stant.

7. Dominōs narrant.

8. Deum laudābātis.

9. Rotam portābitis.

10. Puellās nōn spectābāmus.

F. Answer the following questions.
1. In Latin, what sound does an *ae* make?

2. In words of two syllables, where does the accent fall?

3. To what time does the perfect tense refer?

4. How many endings are there for each tense of a Latin verb?

5. How many declensions are there for Latin nouns?

6. What is the second person singular, imperfect tense ending for *spectō*?

7. What is the first person plural, future tense ending for *vocō*?

8. What is the first person singular, imperfect tense ending for *amō*?

9. What is the third person singular, imperfect tense ending for *dō*?

10. What is the third person plural, future tense ending for *portō*?

EXERCISE FIVE–B

A. Spell out in English how each Latin word should be pronounced and place the accent properly.
  1. agricola
  2. agricolam
  3. poēta
  4. poētās
  5. viārum
  6. discipulōrum
  7. nūntius
  8. nūntiō
  9. gladium
  10. gladiōs

B. Chant each of the following paradigms ten times through.

    ō, s, t! mus, tis, nt!
    amō, amās, amat! amāmus, amātis, amant!
    a, ae, ae, am, ā! ae, ārum, īs, ās, īs!
    us, ī, ō, um, ō! ī, ōrum, īs, ōs, īs!
    um, ī, ō, um, ō! a, ōrum, īs, a, īs!
    bam, bās, bat! bāmus, bātis, bant!
    bō, bis, bit! bimus, bitis, bunt!

C. Translate the following review sentences.

1. Poēta Deum laudābit.

2. Fēminae Deum laudābant.

3. Nautae vocant.

4. Fēminae nautam vocant.

5. Poētae puellās amābant.

6. Poēta et agricola Deum laudābant.

7. Nauta et puella fēminam spectant.

8. Nautae puellam portant.

9. Agricola puellam spectat.

10. Puellās nōn spectābāmus.

D. Translate the following English into Latin.

1. The farmers call.

2. The farmer was calling.

3. The farmers will call.

4. They will call the farmers.

5. They will call the woman.

6. They were calling the women.

7. The sailor carries.

8. The poet will love the woman.

9. The woman looks at the road.

10. The women will look at the road.

11. The flames were ravaging the province.

12. The maid approaches the window, but the window will not change.

13. The farmer labors to change the wall.

14. The sailors were calling the winds.

15. The poet will not tell the rumor.

E. Translate the following Latin into English.
1. Poētae puellās amābant.

2. Poēta Deum laudābit.

3. Nautae vocant.

4. Fēminae nautam vocant.

5. Fēminae Deum laudābant.

6. Agricolae viam spectant.

7. Agricola puellam spectat.

8. Nautae puellam portant.

9. Nauta et puella fēminam spectant.

10. Poēta et agricola Deum laudābant.

11. Fīlius fluvium dēmōnstrābat.

12. Līberī ludōs postulant.

13. Sociī nuntiōs nōn pugnābant.

14. Populī scopulum habitant.

15. Gladium nōn dās.

F. List all the English words you can think of which come from recently studied Latin vocabulary words.

    1.   6.

    2.   7.

    3.   8.

    4.   9.

    5.   10.

G. Answer the following questions.

  1. To what time does the pluperfect tense refer?

  2. How many endings are there for each tense of a Latin verb?

  3. How many case endings are there for each declension of a Latin noun?

  4. What is the third person singular ending, future tense for *spectō*?

  5. What is the second person plural ending, imperfect tense for *vocō*?

  6. Why is it important to learn the genitive singular ending for nouns?

  7. What gender is not found in the Second Declension?

  8. With neuter nouns, which case endings are always the same as one another?

  9. What words have you learned which will not change their endings?

  10. What does *saepe* mean?

SUM: THE VERB OF BEING

Most verbs do something. They run, hit, kick, swim, sit, and so forth. But there is one important verb which does nothing but which shows up a lot regardless. It is the verb of being—*I am, you are*, etc.

In Latin, this verb is irregular. This means that it deviates considerably from the pattern of other verbs. It also means that there is no way to learn it except through separate memorization.

	SINGULAR	PLURAL
FIRST PERSON	*sum*—I am	*sumus*—we are
SECOND PERSON	*es*—you are	*estis*—you are
THIRD PERSON	*est*—he, she, it is	*sunt*—they are

The simplest way to learn this is to chant it just like you chant the other verb endings—*sum, es, est! sumus, estis, sunt!*

THE IMPERFECT TENSE OF SUM

When referring to a time of being in the past, you may use the imperfect tense. It looks like this:

	SINGULAR	PLURAL
FIRST PERSON	*eram*—I was, I used to be	*erāmus*—we were, we used to be
SECOND PERSON	*erās*—you were, you used to be	*erātis*—you were, you used to be
THIRD PERSON	*erat*—he, she, it was, used to be	*erant*—they were, they used to be

This too should be learned as a chant—*eram, erās, erat! erāmus, erātis, erant!*

THE FUTURE TENSE OF SUM

And when referring to the future, sum looks this way:

	SINGULAR	PLURAL
FIRST PERSON	*erō*—I shall be	*erimus*—we shall be
SECOND PERSON	*eris*—you will be	*eritis*—you will be
THIRD PERSON	*erit*—he, she, it will be	*erunt*—they will be

Again, chant them—*erō, eris, erit! erimus, eritis, erunt!*

DOUBLE DUTY

In learning these, you must be careful. This is because later in your study of Latin, you will discover that this is a verb that also serves as a set of endings for something called the *passive voice*, as well as endings for verbs in other tenses.

You do not need to worry about learning this now, but you should remember that there are other applications coming. This can also serve as an incentive to memorize these endings now—it will save you work later on!

EXERCISE SIX

A. Spell out in English how each Latin word should be pronounced and place the accent properly.

1. sum

2. es

3. sunt

4. sumus

5. eram

6. erat

7. erātis

8. erō

9. erunt

10. eritis

B. Chant each of the following paradigms ten times through.

ō, s, t! mus, tis, nt!

amō, amās, amat! amāmus, amātis, amant!

a, ae, ae, am, ā! ae, ārum, īs, ās, īs!

us, ī, ō, um, ō! ī, ōrum, īs, ōs, īs!

um, ī, ō, um, ō! a, ōrum, īs, a, īs!

bam, bās, bat! bāmus, bātis, bant!

bō, bis, bit! bimus, bitis, bunt!

sum, es, est! sumus, estis, sunt!

eram, erās, erat! erāmus, erātis, erant!

erō, eris, erit! erimus, eritis, erunt!

C. Translate the following review sentences.

1. Fīlius fluvium dēmōnstrābat.

2. Līberī ludōs postulant.

3. Sociī nuntiōs nōn pugnābant.

4. Fēminae nautam vocant.

5. Poētae puellās amābant.

6. Poēta et agricola Deum laudābant.

7. Nauta et puella fēminam spectant.

8. Nautae puellam portant.

9. Nauta et puella incolās convocant.

10. Fabulās narrant.

D. Translate the following English into Latin.
   1. You all were.

   2. He was.

   3. I am.

   4. We shall be.

   5. We were.

   6. You are.

   7. You all are.

   8. She will be.

   9. It was.

   10. They are.

E. Translate the following Latin into English.
   1. Nauta est.

   2. Nautae sunt.

   3. Poēta es.

   4. Poētae estis.

   5. Agricola sum.

6. Agricolae sumus.

7. Dōnum est.

8. Vīnum est.

9. Agricolae nōn sumus.

10. Nauta nōn est.

F. Answer the following questions.

1. How many tenses have you learned for the verb of being?

2. What does it mean to say a verb is irregular?

3. What is the third person singular, imperfect tense for *laudō*?

4. What is the third person singular, imperfect tense for *sum*?

5. What is the first person plural, future tense for *sum*?

6. What gender usually fits First Declension nouns?

7. How many declensions are there?

8. How many genders are there for Latin nouns?

9. When translating a Latin sentence, what should you look for first?

10. To what time does the perfect tense refer?

FIRST CONJUGATION: PERFECT TENSE

We are now going to learn the endings for the perfect tense.

	SINGULAR	PLURAL
FIRST PERSON	*laudāvī*—I praised, have praised	*laudāvimus*—we praised, have praised
SECOND PERSON	*laudāvistī*—you praised, have praised	*laudāvistis*—you praised, have praised
THIRD PERSON	*laudāvit*—he, she, it praised, has praised	*laudāvērunt*—they praised, have praised

Learn these the same way you learned the others—*ī, istī, it! imus, istis, ērunt!*

These are the endings which are used to refer to a complete action in the past. But to which part of the verb are they attached? The answer to this question brings us to the Third Principal Part.

Take, for example:

> *laudō, laudāre, laudāvī, laudātum*—praise

The Third Principal Part is *laudāvī*. Notice that the last letter is *-ī*, corresponding to the first person singular ending for the perfect tense. *Laudāvī* means *I praised*. The perfect stem is therefore *laudāv-*. The endings for the perfect tense are attached to this stem.

EXERCISE SEVEN

A. Spell out in English how each Latin word should be pronounced and place the accent properly.

1. laudāvī

2. laudāvistī

3. laudāvit

4. laudāvimus

5. laudāvistis

6. laudāvērunt

7. spectāvī

8. spectāvistī

9. spectāvit

10. spectāvimus

B. Chant each of the following paradigms ten times through.

ō, s, t! mus, tis, nt!

amō, amās, amat! amāmus, amātis, amant!

a, ae, ae, am, ā! ae, ārum, īs, ās, īs!

us, ī, ō, um, ō! ī, ōrum, īs, ōs, īs!

um, ī, ō, um, ō! a, ōrum, īs, a, īs!

bam, bās, bat! bāmus, bātis, bant!
bō, bis, bit! bimus, bitis, bunt!
sum, es, est! sumus, estis, sunt!
eram, erās, erat! erāmus, erātis, erant!
erō, eris, erit! erimus, eritis, erunt!
ī, istī, it! imus, istis, ērunt!

C. Translate the following review sentences.
   1. Fēmina et puella spectant viam.

   2. Poēta Deum laudābit.

   3. Agricola puellam appropinquat.

   4. Deus amābat.

   5. Poēta et agricola equum agitābant.

   6. Nauta et puella fēminam accusant.

   7. Incolae viam dēmōnstrant.

   8. Vīnum spectant.

   9. Dōnum dat.

   10. Dōminī cōnsilium dant.

D. Translate the following English into Latin.
   1. You looked at the girl.

   2. The poet vexed the throng.

   3. The woman and the maidservant praised God.

   4. God loved the world.

   5. The slave carried the sword.

   6. The women delayed the advice.

7. I explored the cave.

8. The friends carried the gifts.

9. We praised the wine.

10. You (pl.) looked at the swords.

E. Translate the following Latin into English.
   1. Spectāvistis.

   2. Deum laudāvistis.

   3. Deum amāvistis.

   4. Deus amāvit.

   5. Deus mundum amāvit.

   6. Portāvērunt.

   7. Gladiōs portāvērunt.

   8. Cōnsilium dedērunt.

   9. Cōnsilium dedit.

   10. Fēminae et puellae vocāvērunt.

F. Answer the following questions.
   1. How many declensions are there for Latin nouns?

   2. How many conjugations are there for Latin verbs?

   3. How many case endings are there for Latin nouns?

   4. How many tenses will we study for Latin verbs?

   5. What are these tenses?

6. What is the third person plural, perfect tense for *vocō?*

7. What is the first person singular, perfect tense for *amō?*

8. What is the second person plural, perfect tense for *spectō?*

9. What is the second person singular, perfect tense for *laudō?*

10. What is the third person singular, perfect tense for *portō?*

FIRST CONJUGATION: PLUPERFECT AND FUTURE PERFECT TENSES

We are now going to learn the endings for the pluperfect tense. You should remember that in the chapter on the verb *sum*, we discussed how the *eram, erās, erat, erāmus, erātis, erant* endings and the *erō, eris, erit, erimus, eritis, erunt* endings would come in handy later. This is the first place where they will. (But only if you did what you were supposed to, and memorized them!)

PLUPERFECT TENSE

The pluperfect tense shows an action completed *prior to* some point in the past. Now here is where it may get slightly confusing. The endings for the *pluperfect* tense are the same as the *imperfect* forms of *sum*. They are: *eram, erās, erat, erāmus, erātis, erant*.

When they stand alone, they mean *I was, you were*, etc. But when they are attached to the perfect stem *(laudāv-)*, they give us the pluperfect tense. Thus:

	SINGULAR	PLURAL
FIRST PERSON	*laudāveram*—I had praised	*laudāverāmus*—we had praised
SECOND PERSON	*laudāverās*—you had praised	*laudāverātis* you had praised
THIRD PERSON	*laudāverat*—he had praised	*laudāverant*—they had praised

FUTURE PERFECT TENSE

Oddly enough, the same sort of thing is done in the formation of the future perfect tense. The future forms of *sum* are *erō, eris, erit, erimus, eritis, erunt*. On their own they mean *I shall be, you will be*, etc. But when they are attached to the perfect stem *(laudāv-)*, they place the verb in the future perfect tense. Like this:

	SINGULAR	PLURAL
FIRST PERSON	*laudāverō*—I shall have praised	*laudāverimus*—we shall have praised
SECOND PERSON	*laudāveris*—you will have praised	*laudāveritis*—you will have praised
THIRD PERSON	*laudāverit*—he will have praised	*laudāverint*—they will have praised

The only difference is seen in the ending for the third person plural. It is *erint* instead *of erunt*. But other than that, you already have this set of endings memorized.

EXERCISE EIGHT

A. Spell out in English how each Latin word should be pronounced and place the accent properly.

1. laudāveram

2. laudāverās

3. laudāverat

4. laudāverāmus

5. laudāverātis

6. laudāverant

7. spectāverō

8. spectāveris

9. spectāverit

10. spectāverimus

B. Chant each of the following paradigms ten times through.

ō, s, t! mus, tis, nt!
bam, bās, bat! bāmus, bātis, bant!
bō, bis, bit! bimus, bitis, bunt!
a, ae, ae, am, ā! ae, ārum, īs, ās, īs!
us, ī, ō, um, ō! ī, ōrum, īs, ōs, īs!
um, ī, ō, um, ō! a, ōrum, īs, a, īs!
sum, es, est! sumus, estis, sunt!
eram, erās, erat! erāmus, erātis, erant!
erō, eris, erit! erimus, eritis, erunt!
ī, istī, it! imus, istis, ērunt!
eram, erās, erat! erāmus, erātis, erant!
erō, eris, erit! erimus, eritis, erint!

C. Translate the following review sentences.

1. Fēmina spectat viam.

2. Poēta laudābit.

3. Agricola gladiōs dēmōnstrat.

4. Deus amābat mundum.

5. Equī campum explorābant.

6. Nauta et puella fēminās convocābant.

7. Famulus praemium mandat.

8. Vīnum portant.

9. Equus agricolam vexat.

10. Dōminī cōnsilium dant.

D. Translate the following English into Latin.
   1. You had looked at the girl.

   2. The girl will have looked at the poet.

   3. The woman and the girl had praised God.

   4. God had loved the world. *Deus amaverat mundum.*

   5. The woman will have given the sword. *Femina dederit gladium.*

   6. The women had given advice. *Feminae dederant*

   7. I shall have praised the advice.

   8. We shall have carried the gifts.

   9. We had praised the wine.

   10. You (pl.) will have looked at the swords.

E. Translate the following Latin into English.
   1. Spectāveram. *I had looked at*

   2. Deum laudāverātis. *You all had praised God.*

   3. Deum amāverō. *I will have loved God.*

   4. Deus amāverat. *God had loved.*

5. Deus mundum amāverat. *God had loved the world.*

6. Portāverant. *They had carried*

7. Gladiōs portāverant.

8. Cōnsilium dederat.

9. Cōnsilium dederit.

10. Fēminae et puellae vocāverint.

F. Answer the following questions.

1. What is the genitive singular case ending for the First Declension?

2. What is the gentive singular case ending for the Second Declension?

3. What is the genitive singular case ending for the Second Declension neuter?

4. To what time does the pluperfect tense refer?

5. To what time does the future perfect tense refer?

6. What is the third person plural, pluperfect tense for *vocō?*

7. What is the first person singular, future perfect tense for *amō?*

8. What is the second person plural, pluperfect tense for *spectō?*

9. What is the second person singular, future perfect tense for *laudō?*

10. What is the third person singular, pluperfect tense for *portō?*

QUESTIONS

In Latin, there are basically three different ways to ask a question. The *first* is a simple question, seeking information. The other two ways are questions which expect an answer, whether yes or *no*. As was mentioned in an earlier chapter, the verb in Latin commonly goes at the end of a sentence. But this is not necessary. One reason it may be found elsewhere in a sentence is through its frequent placement at the beginning of a sentence in a direct question.

The first way to turn a Latin sentence into a question is to place the suffix *-ne* on the end of the first word in the sentence. Take this sentence for example:

Deum laudāmus—We praise God.

Let's turn this into a question:

Laudāmusne Deum?—Do we praise God?

EXPECTING A "NO" ANSWER

Sometimes when we ask a question, we think we know what answer we are going to get. In Latin, there are two words to use to indicate which answer we think we shall receive. When the questioner believes the answer to his question will be *no*, he begins his sentence with the word *num*. The *num* is not used in addition to the suffix *-ne*, it is used instead of it. It would look like this:

Num fēminae poētam amābant?—The women were not loving the poet, were they?

EXPECTING A "YES" ANSWER

But suppose the questioner is more optimistic. He thinks that the answer to his question will be *yes*. The word he must use to express his optimism is *nōnne*. Like *num*, it will be the first word of the sentence, and is used in place of *-ne:*

Nōnne Deum laudāmus?—We praise God, do we not?

EXERCISE NINE

A. Spell out in English how each Latin word should be pronounced and place the accent properly.

1. vocāveram
2. vocāverās
3. vocāverat
4. vocāverāmus
5. vocāverātis
6. vocāverant

7. amāverō

8. amāveris

9. amāverit

10. amāverimus

B. Chant each of the following paradigms ten times through.

ō, s, t! mus, tis, nt!

bam, bās, bat! bāmus, bātis, bant!

bō, bis, bit! bimus, bitis, bunt!

a, ae, ae, am, ā! ae, ārum, īs, ās, īs!

us, ī, ō, um, ō! ī, ōrum, īs, ōs, īs!

um, ī, ō, um, ō! a, ōrum, īs, a, īs!

sum, es, est! sumus, estis, sunt!

eram, erās, erat! erāmus, erātis, erant!

erō, eris, erit! erimus, eritis, erunt!

ī, istī, it! imus, istis, ērunt!

eram, erās, erat! erāmus, erātis, erant!

erō, eris, erit! erimus, eritis, erint!

C. Translate the following review sentences.

1. Fīlius fluvium dēmōnstrābat.

2. Līberī ludōs postulant.

3. Sociī nuntiōs nōn pugnābant.

4. Fēminae nautam vocant.

5. Poētae puellās amābant.

6. Nauta et puella fēminam accusant.

7. Incolae viam dēmōnstrant.

8. Vīnum spectant.

9. Dōnum dat.

10. Dōminī cōnsilium dant.

D. Translate the following English into Latin.

1. Had you looked at the girl?

2. Did the girl look at the poet?

3. Do the woman and the girl praise God? *Laudantne femina et puella Deum*

4. Will God love the world? *Amabitne Deus mundum?*

5. Was the woman giving the sword?

6. Had the women given advice? *dederantne feminae concilium*

7. Shall we have praised the advice? *laudaverimusne concilium*

8. You will have carried the gifts, will you not? *Nonne portaveritis dona?*

9. They had not praised the wine, had they? *Num laudaverant vinum?*

10. You (pl.) looked at the swords, didn't you? *Nonne*

E. Translate the following Latin into English.

1. Spectāveramne?

2. Laudāveratisne Deum?

3. Amāverōne Deum?

4. Amāveratne Deus?

5. Amāveratne Deus mundum?

6. Nōnne spectat?

7. Num laudātis?

8. Nōnne dederat cōnsilium?

9. Num dederit cōnsilium?

10. Vocāverintne fēminae et puellae?

F. Answer the following questions.

1. What is the genitive singular case ending for the Second Declension? *-i*

2. To what time does the imperfect tense refer? *Past Progressive*

3. Why is the genitive singular ending always listed with a noun in the dictionary? *to tell you what declension the noun is in*

4. What is the principal gender for the First Declension? *feminine*

5. What suffix is attached to a word to turn a sentence into a question? *-ne*

6. To which word is the suffix attached? *the verb*

7. What word is used to create a question expecting a *no* for an answer? *num*

8. What word is used to create a question expecting a *yes* for an answer? *nonne*

9. Where are these words placed in the sentence? *at the beginning*

10. What is the third person singular, pluperfect tense, in a question for *portō?* *portaverath*

PREDICATE NOMINATIVE AND APPOSITION

PREDICATE NOMINATIVE

We have already learned that the nominative case is used when a noun is the subject of the sentence. But there is another usage for the nominative case which we call the *predicate nominative*. As may be guessed, it is called this because it occurs when a noun in the predicate, or second part of a sentence, takes the nominative case.

This is how it works. As mentioned before, most verbs do something. Action goes through the verb and *to* the direct object. In Latin, this is shown by placing the direct object in *the accusative* case. But there is another verb which simply shows existence—the verb of being—*sum*.

For purposes of understanding the predicate nominative, consider the verb of being an *equal sign*. When you use an equal sign, it means that whatever is on either side of that sign must be the same. So, 2 + 2 = 4. It is the same with *is* in English, and *sum* in Latin. For example, when someone phones you and asks for Bob, you should not say:

This is him.

Why not? Because even though it is in the predicate, it follows the verb *is*. This means that it should appear in the same form as when it is used as the subject of the sentence. Thus, you say:

This is he. (This = he.)

Now how does this work in Latin? Basically, it works the same way. To see how it works, contrast the following two sentences.

Christus Deum laudat—Christ praises God.
Christus Deus est—Christ is God.

In the second sentence, *Deus* is in the nominative case because the point of the statement is to say that Christ *equals* God. When that equation is not being made, then the the direct object is put in the accusative case.

APPOSITION

Something very similar happens when we see an example of what is called *apposition. This* occurs when a noun is placed alongside another noun to explain it in greater detail. First, an example in English:

Mark, a messenger, loves God.

Here we see that *messenger* is a noun *in apposition* to the proper name *Mark*. We call *messenger* the appositive. In Latin, this relationship is recognized by placing the noun in apposition in the same case as the noun it describes.

Marcus, nūntius, Deum amat.

EXERCISE TEN

A. Spell out in English how each Latin word should be pronounced and place the accent properly.

1. portāvit
2. portāvimus
3. portāvī
4. portant
5. portat
6. portāmus
7. portābunt
8. portābit
9. portābimus
10. portāveram

B. Chant each of the following paradigms ten times through.

ō, s, t! mus, tis, nt!
bam, bās, bat! bāmus, bātis, bant!
bō, bis, bit! bimus, bitis, bunt!
a, ae, ae, am, ā! ae, ārum, īs, ās, īs!
us, ī, ō, um, ō! ī, ōrum, īs, ōs, īs!
um, ī, ō, um, ō! a, ōrum, īs, a, īs!
sum, es, est! sumus, estis, sunt!
eram, erās, erat! erāmus, erātis, erant!
erō, eris, erit! erimus, eritis, erunt!
ī, istī, it! imus, istis, ērunt!
eram, erās, erat! erāmus, erātis, erant!
erō, eris, erit! erimus, eritis, erint!

C. Translate the following review sentences.

1. Mundum Deus amat. *God loves the world.*

2. Spectant. *They look at.*

3. Puellam laudābunt. *They will love the girl.* (praise)

4. Poētae puellās amābant. *The poets were loving the girls.*

5. Deus Fīlium dat. *God gives the son.*

6. Fīlius Deum amat. *The son loves God.*

7. Poētae estis. *You (all) are the poets.*

8. Vīnum est. *It is the wine.*

9. Amāte!

10. Cōnsilium dedērunt.

11. Portāverant.

12. Gladiōs portāverant.

13. Cōnsilium dederat.

14. Cōnsilium dederit.

15. Fēminae et puellae vocāverint.

D. Translate the following English into Latin.

1. Christ is God.

2. Christ praises God.

3. The poet is a sailor.

4. The sailor is a poet.

5. The farmer calls the poet.

6. The settler is a farmer.

7. The settler, a farmer, praises the decision. *Incola, agricola, laudat sententia*

8. The sailor, a poet, praises the farmer. *Nauta, poeta,*

9. The farmers, poets, look at the road. *Agricolae, poetae, spectant viam*

10. The farmers are poets. *Agricolae*

E. Translate the following Latin into English.

1. Fēminae, poētae, Deum amābant.

2. Fēmina, poēta, Deum amāvit.

3. Puella fēmina est.

4. Fēmina est.

5. Sunt fēminae.

6. Fēmina, poēta, agricolam spectāvit

7. Spectāvimus fēminam, poētam

8. Agricolae sunt.

9. Puellae fēminae sunt.

10. Agricolae nautae nōn sunt.

F. Answer the following questions.

1. What gender is not found in the Second Declension?

2. To what time does the present tense refer?

3. What is the third person singular ending, future tense for *spectō*?

4. How many endings are there for each tense of a Latin verb?

5. In words of three syllables, where does the accent fall?

6. What is apposition?

7. What is the predicate nominative?

8. Give an example of the predicate nominative in English.

9. Give an example of the predicate nominative in Latin.

10. What mathematics sign does the verb *is* resemble?

REVIEW OF THE GENITIVE AND DATIVE CASES

We have already discussed the uses of two of the noun cases—nominative and accusative. These cases perform the same function for nouns of all five declensions. Thus far we have studied only the first and second declensions.

You recall that the First Declension case endings look like this:

	SINGULAR	PLURAL
NOMINATIVE	villa	villae
GENITIVE	villae	villārum
DATIVE	villae	villīs
ACCUSATIVE	villam	villās
ABLATIVE	villā	villīs

And the Second Declension Masculine case endings look like this:

	SINGULAR	PLURAL
NOMINATIVE	Deus	Deī
GENITIVE	Deī	Deōrum
DATIVE	Deō	Deīs
ACCUSATIVE	Deum	Deōs
ABLATIVE	Deō	Deīs

You should remember that the case endings for the Second Declension Neuter Nouns are:

	SINGULAR	PLURAL
NOMINATIVE	dōnum	dōna
GENITIVE	dōnī	dōnōrum
DATIVE	dōnō	dōnīs
ACCUSATIVE	dōnum	dōna
ABLATIVE	dōnō	dōnīs

GENITIVE CASE

Remember that the genitive case shows possession. In English, possession may be shown by the word *of* or by an apostrophe. For example: *the woman's son* and *the son of the woman* both represent the same idea. In Latin, a genitive ending is used to show this idea and it would look like this:

fīlius fēminae

Let's take a look at how the genitive case looks when it is used with nouns of the SECOND DECLENSION. Here is a sentence to consider:

The messenger's slaves look at the sword.

Now remember our earlier warning. The subject here is *slaves*. It is plural so it has to be *servī*. Now because the subject is plural, the verb has to be plural also—3rd person plural. It would therefore be *spectant*. What is being looked at? The *sword* would have to be in the accusative case—*gladium*. And coming to the point of this exercise, we must render *messenger's* by putting it in the genitive case—*nūntiī*. (Each *i* is pronounced so it would be *noon ti ee*.)

Servī nūntiī gladium spectant.

If in our English sentence there were many messengers, indicated by an apostrophe after the *s* (*The messengers' slaves . . .*), then we would use the genitive plural. The sentence would then look like this:

> *Servī nūntiōrum gladium spectant.*

DATIVE CASE

The most common use of the *dative case* is to show *to whom* or *for whom* the action of the verb is *told, given, shown,* or *done.* Common verbs in Latin which are accompanied by the Dative case are: *dō, narrō, dēmōnstrō, dīcō,* and *faciō.* In English, this is called the *indirect object.* In the English sentence below, the indirect object is not in italics.

> *The woman gives the* son *a sword.*
> *The woman gives a sword* to the son.

In Latin the way this is shown is to put the word *son* into the dative case. Thus:

> *Fēmina gladium* fīliō *dat.*

In this sentence, *fēmina* is nominative singular, *gladium* is accusative singular, *dat* is the verb, and is third person singular; and *fīliō* is dative singular.

To reinforce a point made earlier, what does this sentence say if we change it to the following?

> *Gladium dat fēmina fīliō.*

Here we have simply rearranged the words. Because we did not change any of the endings of the words, we have not really changed the sentence grammatically. The meaning of the sentence is the same.

EXERCISE ELEVEN

A. Spell out in English how each Latin word should be pronounced and place the accent properly.

    1. agricolārum

    2. filiōrum

    3. poëtae

    4. fēminae

    5. fēminārum

    6. servīs

    7. Deō

    8. deīs

    9. puellae

    10. poētīs

B. Chant each of the following paradigms ten times through.

ō, s, t! mus, tis, nt!
bam, bās, bat! bāmus, bātis, bant!
bō, bis, bit! bimus, bitis, bunt!
a, ae, ae, am, ā! ae, ārum, īs, ās, īs!
us, ī, ō, um, ō! ī, ōrum, īs, ōs, īs!
um, ī, ō, um, ō! a, ōrum, īs, a, īs!
sum, es, est! sumus, estis, sunt!
eram, erās, erat! erāmus, erātis, erant!
erō, eris, erit! erimus, eritis, erunt!
ī, istī, it! imus, istis, ērunt!
eram, erās, erat! erāmus, erātis, erant!
erō, eris, erit! erimus, eritis, erint!

C. Translate the following review sentences.

1. Fēminās spectābant.

2. Poēta laudābit.

3. Fēmina spectābit.

4. Agricola et fēmina puellās laudāvērunt.

5. Puellae et fēminae agricolam laudāverint.

6. Nauta et puella navigābant.

7. Laudāte!

8. Dā!

9. Nautae puellam amābant.

10. Amāmus.

D. Translate the following English into Latin.

1. The son of the sailor praises God.

2. God loved the son of the maidservant.

3. The poet's life was praising God.

4. The Son of God carries the farmer's cares.

5. The son of the woman looks at the window of the farmhouse.

6. The woman's son gives the farmers a gift.

7. The woman's son tells the son of the farmer a legend.

8. The farmer's son gives the woman's son a sword.

feminae servi dant

9. The woman's slaves give the son the sword.

10. The slaves of the women were showing the girl a garden.

Servi feminarum puella hortum demonstrabant!

E. Translate the following Latin into English.

1. Servī fēminārum puellās spectant. *The womans slaves look at the girl*

2. Fīlius agricolae dōnum dat. *The son of the farmer gives a gift.*

3. Fīlium fēminae spectō. *The women look at*

4. Servus agricolae fīlium agricolae spectāvit.

5. Servum agricolae laudāverās.

6. Dantne agricolae gladium fīliō?

7. Fēmina et puella agricolīs dōnum dant.

8. Servus agricolae gladium fīliō agricolae dabit.

9. Praemium servō dabitis.

10. Dōnum Deō dederant.

F. Answer the following questions.

1. What is genitive singular case ending for the Second Declension neuter?

2. What is the genitive plural case ending for the First Declension?

3. What is the genitive plural case ending for the Second Declension?

4. How many declensions are there?

5. How many conjugations are there?

6. Which part is the infinitive of the verb?

7. Which case ending indicates possession?

8. What is dative singular case ending for the Second Declension neuter?

9. What are the case endings for the Second Declension?

10. What the are present tense endings for the First Conjugation?

11. How many principal parts does a Latin verb have?

12. Which part gives the perfect stem of the verb?

13. Which case ending indicates the indirect object?

14. Which word in this sentence should go in the dative case?
   The farmer's son gives the woman's son the gift.
15. What is a predicate nominative?

AGREEMENT OF ADJECTIVES AND NOUNS

In English we can tell that a noun is being modified by an adjective by word placement. The adjective almost always immediately precedes the noun.

> *The girl carries the new book.*

In this sentence the adjective *new* modifies *book*. We know that the book is *new* because of where the adjective is placed. If we moved it in the sentence, we change the meaning of the sentence.

> *The new girl carries the book.*

Now the adjective *new* modifies the noun *girl*.

In Latin the way to identify which noun is modified is by looking at the case endings. An adjective must match the noun it modifies in *gender*, *number*, and *case*. This is not to say that word placement is irrelevant in Latin; in Latin the adjective normally follows the noun it modifies.

GENDER—Is it masculine, feminine, or neuter?

NUMBER—Is it singular or plural?

CASE—Is it nominative, genitive, dative, accusative, or ablative?

The adjective copies the noun. Whatever a *noun* is doing in the sentence will also be seen in the *adjective*. Before we continue, let's first learn some Latin adjectives with endings from the first two declensions.

VOCABULARY

bonus, -a, -um	good
fīdus, -a, -um	faithful
magnus, -a, -um	great, large
novus, -a, -um	new
parvus, -a, -um	little, small
malus, -a, -um	bad, evil

Notice carefully how these adjectives are listed. There are three endings given for each adjective. The first, *-us*, corresponds to the SECOND DECLENSION masculine endings. The second ending, *-a*, corresponds to the FIRST DECLENSION endings. The last, *-um*, corresponds to the *Second Declension* neuter endings. This means that the *us, a, um* represent *masculine, feminine,* and *neuter* endings respectively.

In the paradigm for adjectives below, the left-hand column is masculine, the middle is feminine, and the one on the right is neuter. We will use as our sample the adjective meaning *good—bonus, a, um*.

	MASCULINE	FEMININE	NEUTER
SINGULAR			
NOMINATIVE	bonus	bona	bonum
GENITIVE	bonī	bonae	bonī
DATIVE	bonō	bonae	bonō
ACCUSATIVE	bonum	bonam	bonum
ABLATIVE	bonō	bonā	bonō

PLURAL

NOMINATIVE	bonī	bonae	bona
GENITIVE	bonōrum	bonārum	bonōrum
DATIVE	bonīs	bonīs	bonīs
ACCUSATIVE	bonōs	bonās	bona
ABLATIVE	bonīs	bonīs	bonīs

This is how it works in the formation of a sentence. Look at the following sentence:

The woman carries the sword.

Next look at the Latin translation.

Fēmina gladium portat.

Now let's modify this sentence using the adjective *bonus, a, um*. We will add the adjective *good* to describe the woman.

Fēmina bona gladium portat.

As mentioned above, the adjective *bonus, a, um* must match the noun it modifies in *gender, number,* and *case*. Because in this instance it is modifying *fēmina*, it is therefore *feminine, singular,* and *nominative*. Now let's vary it a little. How would we apply *bonus, a, um* to modify the word for *sword*? *Gladium* is *masculine, singular,* and *accusative*—so our word for *good* must match. So the sentence will look like this:

Fēmina gladium bonum portat.

This may all seem pretty simple, but there are a few things that may trip you up. For example, there are a few nouns where the gender of the noun is not obvious from its ending. We learned that *agricola, poēta,* and *nauta* are all masculine even though they have feminine *First Declension* endings.

Remember that the rule is that adjectives must match in *gender, number,* and *case*. It is *not* that the adjective must match in the appearance of the endings (although many times it will do so). For example, look at the following sentence:

The good farmer carries the sword.

In this case, the sentence would have looked like this:

Agricola bonus gladium portat.

You can see that *bonus* matches *agricola* in *gender* (both masculine), *number* (both singular), and *case* (both nominative).

Vocabulary (First and Second Declension Adjectives)

acūtus, -a, -um	sharp, pointed, intelligent
aeger, aegra, aegrum	sick, feeble
albus, -a, -um	white
arduus, -a, -um	steep, lofty
asper, aspera, asperum	rough, harsh
bonus, -a, -um	good
cārus, -a, -um	dear, beloved
celsus, -a, -um	lofty, high
citus, -a, -um	fast, swift
clarus, -a, -um	clear, brilliant
dēfessus, -a, -um	tired, weary
densus, -a, -um	dense, thick
ferus, -a, -um	fierce
fīdus, -a, -um	faithful
firmus, -a, -um	firm, steadfast
gelidus, -a, -um	cold, like ice
grātus, -a, -um	grateful, pleasing
horrendus, -a, -um	dreadful, awful, fearful
ignārus, -a, -um	ignorant
iūstus, -a, -um	just, right, fair, impartial
laetus, -a, -um	happy, joyful, glad
longinquus, -a, -um	far away, distant
longus, -a, -um	long
magnus, -a, -um	great, large
malus, -a, -um	bad, evil
niger, nigra, nigrum	dark, black
novus, -a, -um	new
obscūrus, -a, -um	hidden, dark
parvus, -a, -um	small, little
perītus, -a, -um	skilled, experienced
prīmus, -a, -um	first, foremost
publicus, -a, -um	public
pulcher, pulchra, pulchrum	beautiful, handsome
quiētus, -a, -um	quiet, at rest, peaceful
raucus, -a, -um	roaring, hoarse
salvus, -a, -um	safe, secure, protected
sevērus, -a, -um	severe, strict, rigid
trepidus, -a, -um	trembling, very frightened
ūmidus, -a, -um	wet, damp, moist

EXERCISE TWELVE

A. Spell out in English how each Latin word should be pronounced and place the accent properly.

1. bonus

2. novārum

3. malīs

4. magnus

5. fīda

6. parvōs

7. fīdī

8. bonōrum

9. magnum

10. mala

B. Chant each of the following paradigms ten times through.

ō, s, t! mus, tis, nt!

bam, bās, bat! bāmus, bātis, bant!

bō, bis, bit! bimus, bitis, bunt!

a, ae, ae, am, ā! ae, ārum, īs, ās, īs!

us, ī, ō, um, ō! ī, ōrum, īs, ōs, īs!

um, ī, ō, um, ō! a, ōrum, īs, a, īs!

sum, es, est! sumus, estis, sunt!

eram, erās, erat! erāmus, erātis, erant!

erō, eris, erit! erimus, eritis, erunt!

ī, istī, it! imus, istis, ērunt!

eram, erās, erat! erāmus, erātis, erant!

erō, eris, erit! erimus, eritis, erint!

C. Translate the following review sentences.

1. Deus Fīlium dat.

2. Poētae estis.

3. Vīnum est.

4. Agricola et fēmina viam spectāverant.

5. Puellae et fēminae Deum rogābunt.

6. Incolae viam dēmonstrābunt.

7. Amāte!

8. Cōnsilium dedērunt.

9. Dōnum dabunt.

10. Deum amātis.

D. Translate the following English into Latin.
   1. The good son praises God.

   2. God loved the faithful sons.

   3. The dear woman's little son was praising God.

   4. God loves the evil woman's happy son.

   5. The quiet son of the trembling woman gives the faithful farmer a beautiful gift.

   6. The grateful maidservant's son gives the fierce farmers a little gift.

   7. The woman's son gives the intelligent son of the farmer a great sword.

   8. The severe farmer's evil son gives the woman's just son a sword.

   9. The woman's steadfast slaves give the handsome son the first sword.

   10. The good slaves of the good woman were giving the good girl a good gift.

E. Translate the following Latin into English.
   1. Agricolae bonī gladium fīliō dant.

   2. Fēminae bonae dōnum puellīs dant.

   3. Fēmina et puella agricolīs dōnum bonum dant.

   4. Dōnum fīliō fēminae parvae dant.

5. Gladium magnum fīlius fēminae dabat.

6. Servus puellae dōnum magnum dedit.

7. Servus fīdus agricolae gladium fīliō agricolae dabit.

8. Dōnum agricolae bonō dabis.

9. Gladium novum fīliō dabitis.

10. Dōnum parvum Deō dederant.

F. List all the English words you can think of which come from this lesson's vocabulary words.
   1.   6.
   2.   7.
   3.   8.
   4.   9.
   5.   10.

G. Answer the following questions.
   1. What question must be answered to determine gender?

   2. What question must be answered to determine number?

   3. What question must be answered to determine case?

   4. What is apposition?

   5. What is the verb of being?

   6. Conjugate the verb of being in the imperfect tense.

   7. Conjugate the verb of being in the future tense.

   8. How must an adjective match the noun it modifies?

   9. Give an example of how an adjective may not match the noun it modifies in *appearance*.

   10. What is the dative, feminine plural form of the adjective *parvus*?

THE ABLATIVE CASE

The Ablative Case does all sorts of things in Latin. If you like you may think of it as the "junk drawer" of case endings. In this chapter, we will list together many of the uses of the ablative. This will make it easier to refer back to when you encounter uses of the ablative later on in your work.

Each use of the ablative has a name of its own. And if you ever get stuck in a translation, you may appeal blindly to the "Ablative of desperation." It won't help with the translation, but you may feel better.

Before we turn to the uses of the ablative case, we should look at another vocabulary list.

VOCABULARY

ā, ab	(with abl.) from, away from
cum	(with abl.) with
dē	(with abl.) down from, concerning, about
ē, ex	(with abl.) out of, from
in	(with abl.) in, on
prō	(with abl.) in front of
sub	(with abl.) at the foot of
ager, agrī, m.	field
amīcitia, -ae, f.	friendship
aqua, -ae, f.	water
bellum, -ī, n.	war
caelum, -ī, n.	sky
memoria, -ae, f.	memory
patria, -ae, f.	fatherland, native country
porta, -ae, f.	gate, door
puer, puerī, m.	boy
terra, -ae f.	land, earth
verbum, -ī, n.	word
vir, virī, m.	man

Now below are listed eight basic uses of the ablative, with an example of each. Each word in the ablative case is underlined, as well as the corresponding part of the English translation.

The ABLATIVE ending without a preposition indicates certain ideas.

1. *Ablative of means:* When some inanimate object is used as an instrument or tool to accomplish something, the ablative case ending is placed on that noun.

> *Servus poētās* gladiō *vulnerat.*
> The slave wounds the poets *by means of a sword.*

2. *Ablative of separation:* When two things are separated or parted, the thing from which you are separated is placed in the ablative case.

> *Deus fēminās* cūrā *liberat.*
> God frees women *from worry.*

3. *Ablative of time when:* When something occurs at a particular time, the time is put in the ablative case.

> *Deum laudātis* tertiā hōrā.
> You praise God *at the third hour.*

4. *Ablative of time within which:* When something occurs during a particular time, the time is placed in the ablative case.

> *Oppidum spectābimus* hōrā.
> We shall see the town *within the hour.*

Other times, the *ablative case* is used *with a preposition* to express an idea.

5. *Ablative of accompaniment:* When someone accompanies someone else, those individuals are put in the ablative case, and the preposition *cum* (with) is also used.

> *Nāvigābimus* cum amīcīs.
> We will sail *with friends.*

6. *Ablative of manner:* When the way someone does something is described with a noun, that noun is put in the ablative case and the preposition *cum* is used. *Cum* may be omitted if an adjective describes the noun, but if *cum* is used it must come between the adjective and the noun.

> Magnō cum gaudiō *dabant.*
> They were giving *with great joy.*

7. *Ablative of place from which:* When a particular place is left, the place left is in the ablative case, and the preposition *ā, ab* (from) is also used.

> *Ab* oppidō *ambulāmus.*
> We walk *from town.*

8. *Ablative of place where:* When something occurs somewhere, that place is put in the ablative case (and a preposition is used).

> In īnsulā *puellae ambulābant.*
> The girls were walking *on the island.*

EXERCISE THIRTEEN

A. Spell out in English how each Latin word should be pronounced and place the accent properly.

    1. ambulātis

    2. nāvigāvī

    3. vulnerō

    4. vulnerās

    5. gaudium

    6. īnsulam

7. amīcōs

8. hōrae

9. liberātus

10. oppidum

B. Chant each of the following paradigms ten times through.

ō, s, t! mus, tis, nt!

bam, bās, bat! bāmus, bātis, bant!

bō, bis, bit! bimus, bitis, bunt!

a, ae, ae, am, ā! ae, ārum, īs, ās, īs!

us, ī, ō, um, ō! ī, ōrum, īs, ōs, īs!

um, ī, ō, um, ō! a, ōrum, īs, a, īs!

sum, es, est! sumus, estis, sunt!

eram, erās, erat! erāmus, erātis, erant!

erō, eris, erit! erimus, eritis, erunt!

ī, istī, it! imus, istis, ērunt!

eram, erās, erat! erāmus, erātis, erant!

erō, eris, erit! erimus, eritis, erint!

C. Translate the following review sentences.

1. Servī fēminārum puellās spectant.

2. Fīlius agricolae dōnum dat.

3. Fīlium fēminae spectō.

4. Servus agricolae fīlium agricolae spectāvit.

5. Servum agricolae laudāverās.

6. Servus puellae dōnum magnum dedit.

7. Servus fīdus agricolae gladium fīliō agricolae dabit.

8. Dōnum agricolae bonō dabis.

9. Gladium novum fīliō dabitis.

10. Dōnum parvum Deō dederant.

D. Translate the following English into Latin.

1. The good son praises God with joy.

2. The faithful son walked with the girl.

3. The woman's son was wounding the farmer with a sword.

4. The evil woman's son walks from town.

5. God freed the son of the good woman from worry. *Deus liberavit filium feminae bonae a cura.*

6. The woman's son gives a little gift to the messenger.

7. The woman's son walks in the town.

8. The farmer's evil son gives the man a sword at the third hour.

9. The woman's faithful slaves carry the sword to the son within the hour.

10. The good slaves of the good women were often walking on the hidden island.

E. Translate the following Latin into English.

1. Agricolae bonī gladium puerō dant hōrā. *The good farmers give the sword to the boy within the hour.*

2. Fēminae bonae ambulābant in īnsulā.

3. Fēmina et puella ambulāvērunt ab oppidō.

4. Amīcitiam fīliō nūntiī fēminae parvae dant.

5. Gladium magnum fīlius fēminae cum gaudiō dabat.

6. Servus puellae agricolam gladiō magnō vulnerāvit. *Acc Da/Ab Da/Ab he wounds*

7. Servus fīdus agricolae gladium fīliō agricolae hōrā dabit.

8. Deus agricolam liberat cūrā.

9. Cum amīcīs nāvigābāmus.

10. Servus agricolam gladiō vulnerat.

F. Answer the following questions.

1. What is the ablative of manner?

2. What is the ablative of time within which?

3. What is the case which shows possession?

4. What is the ablative of separation?

5. What is the ablative place where?

6. What is the ablative of time when?

7. What is the ablative of means?

8. What is the ablative of accompaniment?

9. What is the ablative of place from which?

10. What is the fourth principal part of the verb *ambulō*?

PREPOSITIONS

Prepositions are words that help to describe relationships. In English, the use of the preposition does not affect the form of the noun which is the *object* of the preposition. For example, consider these prepositional phrases in English, and note how the only thing that varies is the preposition itself:

> . . . in the town
> . . . by the town
> . . . toward the town

But in Latin, when a preposition is used, the noun which is the object of that preposition will usually take the accusative or ablative case. There are also some prepositions which vary in their meaning, depending upon which case follows the preposition. For example, *in* means *in* or *on* when it is followed by the *ablative*, but means *into* when it is followed by the *accusative*.

Some common Latin prepositions are listed below. It is not only important to learn what they mean, but it is also important to memorize what case each preposition takes.

The prepositions with two forms (*ā, ab* for example) are very similar to the English article *a* or *an*. In English, we say *a truck* and *an owl*. The reason for the difference is the fact that the word following *a* begins with a consonant, and the word following *an* begins with a vowel. It is the same with *ā* and *ab*, and *ē* and *ex*. If the word following these prepositions begins with a vowel, then use the preposition that ends with a consonant.

VOCABULARY
ACCUSATIVE CASE
> *ad*—to, near, toward
>> *ad viam*—toward the road
>
> *ante*—before
>> *ante bellum*—before the war
>
> *apud*—among, near, at the house of, in the presence of
>> *apud fīlium*—at the house of the son
>
> *circā*—about, around
>> *circā oppidum*—around the town
>
> *circum*—around, about
>> *circum dōnum*—around the gift
>
> *contrā*—against, opposite
>> *contrā puerum*—against the boy
>
> *in*—into
>> *in oppidum*—into the town
>
> *inter*—between, among
>> *inter feminās*—among the women
>
> *ob*—because of, on account of
>> *ob gladium*—because of the sword

per—through, across, by, by means of
    per viam—by means of the road
post—behind, after
    post murum—behind the wall
prope—near
    prope mensam—near the table
propter—on account of
    propter nuntium—on account of the messenger
sub—close under, under, to the foot of
    sub aquam—under the water
super—over, above
    super discipulum—over the student
trāns—over, across
    trāns agrōs—across the fields

ABLATIVE CASE
    ā, ab—from, away from
        ab oppidō—away from town
    cum—with
        cum amīcō—with a friend
    dē—down from, about, from, concerning
        dē dōnō—concerning the gift
    ē, ex—out of, from
        ex oppidō—out of the town
    in—in, on
        in īnsulā—on the island
    prō—in front of
        prō fēminā —in front of the women
    sub—at the foot of
        sub colle—at the foot of the hill

EXERCISE FOURTEEN

A. Spell out in English how each Latin word should be pronounced and place the accent properly.

    1. prō
    2. ab
    3. dē
    4. ex
    5. sub

6. in

7. cum

8. apud

9. inter

10. propter

B. Chant each of the following paradigms ten times through.

ō, s, t! mus, tis, nt!
bam, bās, bat! bāmus, bātis, bant!
bō, bis, bit! bimus, bitis, bunt!
a, ae, ae, am, ā! ae, ārum, īs, ās, īs!
us, ī, ō, um, ō! ī, ōrum, īs, ōs, īs!
um, ī, ō, um, ō! a, ōrum, īs, a, īs!
sum, es, est! sumus, estis, sunt!
eram, erās, erat! erāmus, erātis, erant!
erō, eris, erit! erimus, eritis, erunt!
ī, istī, it! imus, istis, ērunt!
eram, erās, erat! erāmus, erātis, erant!
erō, eris, erit! erimus, eritis, erint!

C. Translate the following review sentences.

1. Fīlium laudat.

2. Nautae estis.

3. Vīnum bonum dant.

4. Agricola bonus et fēmina bona viam spectāverant.

5. Puellae parvae Deum amābunt.

6. Spectant et laudant.

7. Ambulāte!

8. Cōnsilium bonum dedit.

9. Dōnum bonum dabat.

10. Deum magnum laudās.

D. Translate the following English into Latin.

1. She walks among the women.

2. The faithful man walked toward the road.

3. The woman's son was walking on account of the messenger.

4. The evil woman's son will walk across the field.

5. God freed the son of the good woman from worry.

6. The master told the boy a long story about the wind.

7. The woman's son will walk in front of the sailors.

8. The farmer's evil son carries a sword near the table.

feminae fidi servi spectant gladium apud laeti viri

9. The woman's faithful slaves look at the sword at the house of the happy man.

defessi servi bonarum feminarum ambulabant per oppidum longiquum.

10. The tired slaves of the good women were walking through the distant town.

E. Translate the following Latin into English.

1. Agricolae bonī ambulant ad viam.

2. Fēminae bonae ambulāvērunt in īnsulā.

3. Fēmina et puella ambulāverint ab oppidō.

4. Fēminae parvae inter puellās ambulant.

5. Gladium magnum fīlius fēminae ab oppidō portābat.

6. Servus puellae circā agricolam ambulāverit.

7. Servus fīdus gladium post mūrum portat.

8. Ambulāvimus in oppidum.

9. Nāvigābāmus ad īnsulam.

10. Servī agricolam trāns agrōs portant.

F. List all the English words you can think of which come from this lesson's vocabulary words.

1.   6.

2.   7.

3.   8.

4.   9.

5.   10.

G. Answer the following questions.

1. What case does *trāns* take?

2. How many declensions are there?

3. What is genitive singular ending for the Second Declension?

4. What case does *prope* take?

5. What case does *contrā* take?

6. What does *in* mean with the ablative case?

7. What case does *ab* take?

8. What case does *prō* take?

9. What does *sub* mean with the ablative case?

10. What case does *dē* take?

SECOND CONJUGATION:
PRESENT, IMPERFECT, AND FUTURE TENSES

We come now to the second family of verbs, called the Second Conjugation. We will begin our study of the Second Conjugation by looking at the three tenses that are built off the present stem.

    You should remember that the present tense of a verb represents action as occuring *right now*. We will begin with the present tense of a Second Conjugation verb meaning *to see*—*video*. Let's walk through the present tense for this verb.

	SINGULAR	PLURAL
FIRST PERSON	*video*—I see	*vidēmus*—we see
SECOND PERSON	*vidēs*—you see	*vidētis*—you see
THIRD PERSON	*videt*—he, she, or it sees	*vident*—they see

    Now you have already memorized the conjugational endings for the present tense—*ō, s, t! mus, tis, nt!* In the Second Conjugation, these same endings are placed on the stem of the verb (*vidē*) to form the various combinations.

DICTIONARY

When you look up a Second Conjugation verb, you will look it up the same way you do with First Conjugation verbs—through its singular form for the first person. For this verb, you would look up *video*.

    Following *video*, you will see the other three Principal Parts. As with the First Conjugation, the stem is found in the second form. It looks like this:

    video, vidēre, vīdī, vīsum

    The second form here (*vidēre*) is the infinitive of the verb. The stem is found by dropping the *-re* from the end, just like the First Conjugation. This gives you *vidē*—the stem. This is the part of the verb you will use to build all the various forms you will need for the present, imperfect and future tenses.

VOCABULARY

All the verbs in this vocabulary list are Second Conjugation verbs. They are listed with Four Principal Parts:

video, -ēre, vīdī, vīsum	to see
moneō, -ēre, monuī, monitum	to warn
habeō, -ēre, habuī, habitum	to have
prohibeō, -ēre, prohibuī, prohibitum	to prohibit, to keep back

REVIEW VOCABULARY

caleō, -ēre, -uī, -itum	to be hot, be warm, glow
compleō, -ēre, complevī, complētum	to fill, fill up

iaceō, -ēre, -uī, - - - -   to lie (flat)
impendeō, -ēre, impendī, impensum   to threaten, hang over
placeō, -ēre, -uī, -itum   to please (be pleasing to)
terreō, -ēre, -uī, -itum   to frighten

In order to conjugate these verbs in the present tense, simply attach the endings (*ō*, *s*, *t*, *mus*, *tis*, *nt*) to the stem. Thus, for example:

> *videō, vidēs, videt, vidēmus, vidētis, vident*
> *moneō, monēs, monet, monēmus, monētis, monent*

IMPERFECT TENSE

Now we will move on to the imperfect and future tenses. Because of this, we will be building off the same stem. As before we will be using *video* for our example.

The imperfect endings are the same as in the First Conjugation:

> *bam, bās, bat! bāmus, bātis, bant!*

You should remember that the stem for *video* is *vidē*. We therefore will conjugate this verb in the imperfect tense this way:

	SINGULAR	PLURAL
FIRST PERSON	*vidēbam*—I was seeing	*vidēbāmus*—we were seeing
SECOND PERSON	*vidēbās*—you were seeing	*vidēbātis*—you were seeing
THIRD PERSON	*vidēbat*—he, she or it was seeing	*vidēbant*—they were seeing

FUTURE TENSE

In the Second Conjugation, the endings for the future tense are the same as for the First Conjugation:

> *bō, bis, bit! bimus, bitis, bunt!*

When they are attached to the stem of the verb *video*, it looks this way:

	SINGULAR	PLURAL
FIRST PERSON	*vidēbō*—I will see	*vidēbimus*—we will see
SECOND PERSON	*vidēbis*—you will see	*vidēbitis*—you will see
THIRD PERSON	*vidēbit*—he, she or it will see	*vidēbunt*—they will see

EXERCISE FIFTEEN

A. Spell out in English how each Latin word should be pronounced and place the accent properly.

    1. prohibeō

    2. videō

    3. videt

    4. vidētis

    5. habet

    6. habēmus

    7. habēbit

    8. prohibēbāmus

    9. vidēbunt

    10. vidēbant

B. Chant each of the following paradigms ten times through.

    ō, s, t! mus, tis, nt!

    bam, bās, bat! bāmus, bātis, bant!

    bō, bis, bit! bimus, bitis, bunt!

    a, ae, ae, am, ā! ae, ārum, īs, ās, īs!

    us, ī, ō, um, ō! ī, ōrum, īs, ōs, īs!

    um, ī, ō, um, ō! a, ōrum, īs, a, īs!

    sum, es, est! sumus, estis, sunt!

    eram, erās, erat! erāmus, erātis, erant!

    erō, eris, erit! erimus, eritis, erunt!

    ī, istī, it! imus, istis, ērunt!

    eram, erās, erat! erāmus, erātis, erant!

    erō, eris, erit! erimus, eritis, erint!

C. Write the four principal parts of the following verbs. Then chant each verb "set" ten times through.

    vocō

    stō

    habeō

    moneō

    videō

D. Translate the following review sentences.

1. Fīliōs laudat.

2. Nautae estis.

3. Vīnum malum dant.

4. Agricola bonus et fēmina bona gladium spectāverant.

5. Puellae parvae Deum amābunt et laudābunt.

6. Spectat et laudat.

7. Ambulā!

8. Cōnsilium malum dedit.

9. Dōnum parvum dabat.

10. Deum magnum laudātis.

E. Translate the following English into Latin.

1. He frightens the women.

2. Does the faithful son see the road?

3. The woman's son was warning the messenger.

4. The terrified woman's son will see the hidden road.

5. God warns the son of the good woman.

6. The woman's son has a little gift.

7. The woman's son was warning the sailors.

8. The farmer's evil son has a sword near the table, hasn't he?

9. The woman's faithful slaves see the sword at the house of the man.

10. The bad slaves of the good women were walking.

F. Translate the following Latin into English.

    1. Vidēmus viam.

    2. Nautās prohibēmus.

    3. Gladius fēminam terret.

    4. Silvae tenebrās habent.

    5. Gladium magnum fīlius fēminae vidēbat.

    6. Servum puellae vidēbitis.

    7. Servus fīdus gladium vidēbat.

    8. Perīculī oppidum impendent.

    9. Copiae fēminam prohibent.

    10. Agricolae carrōs complēbunt.

G. List all the English words you can think of which come from this lesson's **vocabulary words**.

1.	6.
2.	7.
3.	8.
4.	9.
5.	10.

H. Answer the following questions.

    1. What case does *sub* take?

    2. How many conjugations are there?

    3. What is the genitive plural ending for the Second Declension?

    4. What case does *post* take?

    5. What case does *in* take?

6. How is the stem for the Second Conjugation found?

7. Are the endings for the imperfect tense the same for the First and Second Conjugations?

8. What are the endings for the future tense in the Second Conjugation?

9. How would one command more than one person *to see*?

10. What is the second person, plural ending, imperfect tense for the verb *video*?

READING ONE

If you have been faithful to memorize your vocabulary lists as they were given in the lessons, you will enjoy reading in the Latin language. At first, read through the whole selection. Get the main idea. Then you may wish to do a verbatim (word by word) translation or a syntax analysis to better understand the selection or the author's style of writing.

Just as you may have favorite authors, or perhaps favorite kinds of genre or style in English, so you may find some Latin authors or stories you prefer more than others. The more you learn about the Latin language, the more opportunities you will have to pursue your own interests in your reading.

PECUNIA OBSCURA

Puerī et puellae prope harēnam ambulābant. Parvam īnsulam vidēbant. Nautae famās dē pecūniā latebrā in īnsulā narrāvērunt. Līberī laetī semper amābant explorāre. Altē cōgitāvērunt. Mox carrum appropinquāvērunt et laborāvērunt. Rotās ā carrō removērunt. Tum carrum sine rotīs in aquam locāvērunt. Ad insulam navigāvērunt. Terram cum diligentiā spectāvērunt. Dēmōnstrābitne insula līberīs latebram argentī?

VOCABULARY FOR THIS STORY:

altē	(adv.) deeply
cōgitō, -āre, -āvī, -ātum	to turn over in the mind, consider, think, reflect
diligentia, -ae, f., diligence	care
locō, -āre, -āvī, -ātum	to place, put, set
mox	(adv.) soon
removeō, -ēre,-mōvī, -mōtum	to remove, withdraw
sine	(prep. with abl.) without
tum	(adv.) then

VOCABULARY FOR ASKING QUESTIONS:

cūr	why?
ubi	where?

QUESTIONS

After you have read the story, (go ahead, read it aloud!) answer these questions orally in complete sentences.

COMPREHENSION:

1. Ubi līberī ambulābant?

2. Cūr altē cōgitāvērunt?

3. Ubi puerī et puellae navigāvērunt?

GRAMMAR:

Give the case and the reason for the use of that case for the following nouns:

    1. (line 1) pecūniā

    2. (line 2) laetī

    3. (line 2) carrum

    4. (line 3) rotīs

    5. (line 5) diligentiā

SECOND CONJUGATION:
PERFECT, PLUPERFECT, AND FUTURE PERFECT

In the Second Conjugation there are three tenses that are built off the *Third Principal Part*—just as in the First Conjugation. The three tenses that are built off the perfect stem are the perfect, pluperfect, and future perfect tenses.

PERFECT TENSE

You should remember that the perfect tense of a verb represents action as completed at a point in time *in the past*. We will begin with the perfect tense of the same Second Conjugation verb we used in the last chapter—*video*. The endings for the perfect tense are the same as in the First Conjugation—*ī, istī, it*, etc.. The perfect tense for this verb looks this way:

	SINGULAR	PLURAL
FIRST PERSON	*vīdī*—I saw, have seen	*vīdimus*—we saw, have seen
SECOND PERSON	*vīdistī*—you saw, have seen	*vīdistis*—you saw, have seen
THIRD PERSON	*vīdit*—he, she, or it saw, has seen	*vīdērunt*—they saw, have seen

VOCABULARY

The words here are the same as in the last chapter. Notice that the Third Principal Part is underlined. This is the part used for the formation of the perfect, pluperfect, and future perfect.

video, -ēre, vīdī, vīsum	to see
moneō, -ēre, monuī, monitum	to warn
habeō, -ēre, habuī, habitum	to have
prohibeō, -ēre, prohibuī, prohibitum	to prohibit

In order to conjugate one of these verbs in the perfect tense, simply attach the appropriate endings (*ī, istī, it, imus, istis, ērunt*) to the perfect stem. Thus, for example:

monuī, monuistī, monuit, monuimus, monuistis, monuērunt

PLUPERFECT TENSE

Now we will move on to the pluperfect and future perfect tenses. We are still building off the same perfect stem—the Third Principal Part. As before we will be using *video* for our example.

The pluperfect endings are the same as in the First Conjugation:

eram, erās, erat! erāmus, erātis, erant!

You should remember that the perfect stem for *video* is *vīd*. We therefore will conjugate this verb in the pluperfect tense this way:

	SINGULAR	PLURAL
FIRST PERSON	*vīderam*—I had seen	*vīderāmus*—we had seen
SECOND PERSON	*vīderās*—you had seen	*vīderātis*—you had seen
THIRD PERSON	*vīderat*—he, she or it had seen	*vīderant*—they had seen

FUTURE PERFECT TENSE

In the Second Conjugation, the endings for the future tense are the same as for the First Conjugation:

erō, eris, erit! erimus, eritis, erint!

When they are attached to the perfect stem of the verb *video*, it looks this way:

	SINGULAR	PLURAL
FIRST PERSON	*vīderō*—I shall have seen	*vīderimus*—we shall have seen
SECOND PERSON	*vīderis*—you will have seen	*vīderitis*—you will have seen
THIRD PERSON	*vīderit*—he, she, it will have seen	*vīderint*—they will have seen

EXERCISE SIXTEEN

A. Spell out in English how each Latin word should be pronounced and place the accent properly.

1. monuī
2. vīdī
3. habuī
4. prohibuī
5. monuistī
6. habuistis
7. vīdistis
8. prohibuērunt
9. vīderam
10. vīderō

B. Chant each of the following paradigms five times through.

ō, s, t! mus, tis, nt!
bam, bās, bat! bāmus, bātis, bant!
bō, bis, bit! bimus, bitis, bunt!
a, ae, ae, am, ā! ae, ārum, īs, ās, īs!
us, ī, ō, um, ō! ī, ōrum, īs, ōs, īs!
um, ī, ō, um, ō! a, ōrum, īs, a, īs!
sum, es, est! sumus, estis, sunt!
eram, erās, erat! erāmus, erātis, erant!
erō, eris, erit! erimus, eritis, erunt!
ī, istī, it! imus, istis, ērunt!
eram, erās, erat! erāmus, erātis, erant!
erō, eris, erit! erimus, eritis, erint!

C. Write the four principal parts of the following verbs. Then chant each verb "set" ten times through.

amō
clamō
caleō
compleō
iaceō

D. Decline:

mensa

servus

antrum

E. Conjugate:

vocō

videō

F. Translate the following review sentences.

1. Fīliōs videō.

2. Nautās vidēs.

3. Fēmina et puella ambulāverint ab oppidō.

4. Fēminae parvae inter puellās ambulant.

5. Gladium magnum fīlius fēminae ab oppidō portābat.

6. Servus puellae circā agricolam ambulāverit.

7. Servus fīdus gladium post mūrum portat.

8. Cōnsilium malum dabit.

9. Dōnum parvum dabunt.

10. Deum magnum laudās.

G. Translate the following English into Latin.
   1. She saw the women with a man.

   2. The faithful son had seen the road.

   3. The woman's son warned the messenger about the danger.

   4. The evil woman's son will have seen the road within the hour.

   5. God warned the son of the good woman.

   6. The woman's son had a little gift.

   7. The woman's son saw the sailors near the cave.

   8. The farmer's evil son will have had a sword on the table.

   9. The woman's faithful slaves had seen the sword at the house of the son.

   10. The bad slaves of the good women walked.

H. Translate the following Latin into English.
   1. Vīdimus viam ad antrum.

   2. Nautās prohibuī.

   3. Laeta fēmina gladium habuit.

   4. Fēminae bonum vīnum habuērunt.

5. Fīlius fēminae gladium magnum vīdit.

6. Servus puellae propter flammam caluerit.

7. Gladius servum fīdum placuit.

8. Vīdistisne ē fenestrā oppidum?

9. Servus fēminam prohibuerat.

10. Servī agricolam monuērunt.

I. Answer the following questions.

1. What is the accusative plural form of *dōnum*?

2. What is the genitive singular ending for the Second Declension?

3. What is genitive singular ending for the First Declension?

4. What case does *circā* take?

5. What does *in* mean when it is followed by the accusative?

6. What is the third principal part for the verb *videō*?

7. Are the endings for the pluperfect tense the same for the First and Second Conjugations?

8. What are the endings for the future perfect tense in the Second Conjugation?

9. How would one command more than one person *to warn*?

10. What is the second person, plural ending, future perfect tense for the verb *videō*?

GIVING A SYNOPSIS OF A VERB

You have already learned to conjugate verbs from the First and Second Conjugation, and you have learned to do so in six tenses—present, imperfect, future, perfect, pluperfect, and future perfect. No small accomplishment!

But there is more to learn. In this chapter you will learn to give a *synopsis* of a verb. A synopsis is when you give, for a particular verb, an example of the same person and number from the different tenses.

Say, for example, you were asked to give a synopsis for the verb *laudō*. You would be asked to do so in this way:

laudō in the third person singular

This means that you are to give the third person singular form for all six tenses you have learned. It would look like this:

laudat—he praises
laudābat—he was praising
laudābit—he will be praising
laudāvit—he praised, he has praised
laudāverat—he had praised
laudāverit—he will have praised

Or you might be asked to give a synopsis for the verb *videō*.

videō in the second person plural
vidētis—you see
vidēbātis—you were seeing
vidēbitis—you will see
vīdistis—you saw, you have seen
vīderātis—you had seen
vīderitis—you will have seen

EXERCISE SEVENTEEN

A. Spell out in English how each Latin word should be pronounced and place the accent properly.

1. monuit

2. vīdimus

3. habuērunt

4. prohibuistī

5. monuī

6. habuistī

7. vīdī

8. prohibuī

9. vīderās

10. vīderit

B. Chant each of the following paradigms five times through.

ō, s, t! mus, tis, nt!
bam, bās, bat! bāmus, bātis, bant!
bō, bis, bit! bimus, bitis, bunt!
a, ae, ae, am, ā! ae, ārum, īs, ās, īs!
us, ī, ō, um, ō! ī, ōrum, īs, ōs, īs!
um, ī, ō, um, ō! a, ōrum, īs, a, īs!
sum, es, est! sumus, estis, sunt!
eram, erās, erat! erāmus, erātis, erant!
erō, eris, erit! erimus, eritis, erunt!
ī, istī, it! imus, istis, ērunt!
eram, erās, erat! erāmus, erātis, erant!
erō, eris, erit! erimus, eritis, erint!

C. Write the four principal parts of the following verbs. Then chant each verb "set" ten times through.

conciliō
conservō
dō
impendeō
placeō

D. Decline:

cūra

vir

novum vallum

Challenge:

bonus agricola

E. Translate the following review sentences.

1. Fīliōs vīdī.

2. Nautās vīdistī.

3. Vīnum habuī.

4. Agricola malus et fēmina parva gladium vidēbunt.

5. Puellae parvae Deum amāvērunt.

6. Spectāvimus et laudāvimus.

7. Amāte!

8. Cōnsilium malum dedit.

9. Dōnum parvum dabant.

10. Deum magnum laudātis.

F. Translate the following English into Latin.

1. She saw the women with many dishes.

2. Soon the faithful son had seen the long road.

3. Then the woman's son will have warned the messenger.

4. The evil woman's son saw the great sword in the dark cave.

5. God will warn the good son of the faithful woman.

6. The woman's son carried wine to the table.

7. The messenger will have seen the sailors with the money.

8. The farmer's good son had a great sword near the door.

9. The woman's faithful slaves had seen the sword of the son.

10. The good slaves of the bad women always walked with great care in the town.

G. Translate the following Latin into English.

   1. Vīdī viam.

   2. Nautās prohibuit.

   3. Fēminae gladium habuērunt.

   4. Fēminae vīnum habuerint.

   5. Gladium magnum fīlius fēminae vīderit.

   6. Servus puellae vīderat.

   7. Servus fīdus gladium videt.

   8. Vīdistis oppida.

   9. Servus feminās prohibuerit.

   10. Servī agricolās vīderint.

H. Give a synopsis of the following verbs.

   1. *videō*—third person, singular

   2. *laudō*—second person, plural

   3. *ambulō*—first person, singular

4. *portō*—third person, plural

5. *dō*—second person, singular

6. *habeō*—first person, plural

I. Answer the following questions.

1. What is the accusative plural form of *oppidum*?

2. What is the genitive singular ending for the First Declension?

3. What is dative plural ending for the Second Declension?

4. What case does *apud* take?

5. What does *in* mean when it is followed by the ablative?

6. What is the third principal part for the verb *dō*?

7. What do you do when you give a synopsis of a verb?

8. What do you do when you conjugate a verb?

9. How would one command just one person to *love*?

10. What is the first person, plural ending, future perfect tense for the verb *habeō*?

READING TWO

In the next lesson you will be learning a new set of noun endings. A few of the words in the following passage have unfamiliar endings, but you will be able to tell their meaning from their similarity to an English derivative and from their place in the sentence. *Eum* (him) and *eius* (his) are pronoun forms which you will learn later in this text.

PSALMUS 150

[1]Alleluia.
Laudāte Dominum in sanctīs eius;
Laudāte eum in firmamentō virtūtis eius.
[2] Laudāte eum in virtūtibus eius,
Laudāte eum secundum multitūdinem magnitūdinis eius.
[3] Laudāte eum in sonō tubae;
Laudāte eum in psalteriō et citharā.
[4] Laudāte eum in tympanō et chorō;
Laudāte eum in chordīs et organō.
[5] Laudāte eum in cymbalīs benesonantibus;
Laudāte eum in cymbalīs iubilationis.
[6] Omnis spiritus [laudāte] Dominum! Alleluia.

QUESTIONS:

1. What form of the verb is *laudāte*?

2. In this passage, what is the best translation of *in* (verses 3-5)?

3. What case is used for all the instruments in verses 4 and 5? Why is this case used?

CHALLENGE:

Look up this psalm in several translations of the Bible. How are the translations different? Which translation most closely matches this Latin version?

THIRD DECLENSION

For the most part, the nouns of the first two declensions can be identified through their endings. With just a few exceptions, First Declension nouns are all feminine. Second Declension nouns are masculine or neuter, with the neuter nouns distinguished by variant endings in the nominative and accusative cases.

Starting with the Third Declension, it will not be as easy to identify the gender of the noun simply by looking at it. Whether or not a Third Declension noun is masculine, feminine, or neuter cannot be determined through the case endings. For this reason, you should *take special care to memorize the gender of each noun as you learn the noun.*

Another interesting feature of the Third Declension is that there is no standard ending for the first case ending—the nominative singular. As you memorize the case endings for this declension, you will memorize *-is* as the ending for the nominative singular ending, but you should be aware that the nominative singular of this declension is highly irregular. Sometimes the *-is* will be there, and sometimes it will not be.

So the way to identify whether or not a noun belongs to the Third Declension is through looking at the genitive singular ending. In the Third Declension, the genitive singular ending is always *-is*.

	SINGULAR	PLURAL
NOMINATIVE	pater	patr*ēs*
GENITIVE	patr*is*	patr*um*
DATIVE	patr*ī*	patr*ibus*
ACCUSATIVE	patr*em*	patr*ēs*
ABLATIVE	patr*e*	patr*ibus*

VOCABULARY

In this vocabulary list, all the nouns belong to the THIRD DECLENSION. Notice particularly the genitive singular ending for each—it is this that identifies the noun as belonging to the Third Declension. Notice the irregularity of the nominative singular endings (*-er, -x, -is*) and the constancy of the genitive singular.

REVIEW VOCABULARY

arbor, arboris, f.	tree
auctōritās, auctōritātis, f.	authority, influence
bōs, bovis, m./f.	cow, bull, ox, (pl.) cattle
coniunx, conjugis, m./f.	husband or wife
custōs, custōdis, m.	guard, watchman
dux, ducis, m.	leader
explōrātor, explōrātōris, m.	scout
flōs, flōris, m.	flower
grex, gregis, m.	herd, flock of sheep
hospes, hospitis, m./f.	guest, stranger; host
lapis, lapidis, m.	stone
laus, laudis, f.	praise
legiō, legiōnis, f.	legion
leō, leōnis, m.	lion
lēx, lēgis, f.	law
lūx, lūcis, f.	light
māter, mātris, f.	mother
mercātor, mercatōris, m.	merchant, trader
mulier, mulieris, f.	woman
nepōs, nepōtis, m.	grandson, descendant
palūs, palūdis, f.	swamp, bog
pastor, pastōris, m.	shepherd
pater, patris, m.	father
rēx, rēgis, m.	king
saepes, saepis, f.	fence, hedge
senex, senis, m.	old man
tempestās, tempestātis, f.	storm
virgō, virginis, f.	maiden, young woman
virtūs, virtūtis, f.	strength, courage, manliness

I-STEMS

Some Third Declension nouns have a quirk worth noting here. They are distinguished by an *-ium* ending in the genitive plural instead of a simple *-um* ending. Third Declension nouns which do this are called Third Declension I-Stems.

RULES FOR IDENTIFYING I-STEMS

If the distinctive ending for the I-Stem is the genitive singular, and that is not given in a dictionary listing, then how is it possible to learn whether a noun is an I-Stem or not? There are three basic categories to remember. All Third Declension I-Stem nouns will fall into one of three classes:

1. If the base of a noun ends with two consonants (with the exception of *tr*), then the nouns is an I-Stem.

2. If the noun is masculine or feminine, and the nominative singular ends with *-is* or *-es*, and if the gentive singular has no more syllables than the nominative singular, then the noun is an I-Stem.

3. If the noun is a neuter noun of the Third Declension and its nominative singular ends in *-al* or *-e*, the noun is an I-stem. (Third Declension Neuter nouns will be discussed in the next lesson.)

Third Declension Masculine and Feminine I-Stems look like this:

	SINGULAR	PLURAL
NOMINATIVE	ign*is*	ign*ēs*
GENITIVE	ign*is*	ign*ium*
DATIVE	ign*ī*	ign*ibus*
ACCUSATIVE	ign*em*	ign*ēs*
ABLATIVE	ign*e*	ign*ibus*

VOCABULARY (I-STEM)

adulēscēns, adulēscēntis*, m.	young man, youth
avis, avis*, f.	bird
canis, canis*, m./f.	dog
collis, collis*, m.	hill
fōns, fontis*, m.	fountain, spring
ignis, ignis*, f.	fire
iuvenis, iuvenis*, m./f.	young person
mōns, montis*, m.	mountain
mors, mortis*, f.	death
nāvis, nāvis*, f.	ship
nox, noctis*, f.	night
ovis, ovis*, f.	sheep
turris, turris*, f.	tower, turret (turrim in accusative singular)
urbs, urbis*, f.	city
vallēs, vallis*, f.	valley, vale
vestis, vestis*, f.	garment, clothing

*=i-stem noun

EXERCISE EIGHTEEN

A. Spell out in English how each Latin word should be pronounced and place the accent properly.

  1. mātris
  2. lūcibus
  3. patrem
  4. mātrēs
  5. rēgibus
  6. lēgibus
  7. lēge
  8. patribus
  9. mātrum
  10. montibus

B. Chant each of the following paradigms ten times through.

  is, is, ī, em, e! ēs, um, ibus, ēs, ibus!
  ī, istī, it! imus, istis, ērunt!
  eram, erās, erat! erāmus, erātis, erant!
  erō, eris, erit! erimus, eritis, ērint!

C. Chant each of the following paradigms two times through.

  ō, s, t! mus, tis, nt!
  bam, bās, bat! bāmus, bātis, bant!
  bō, bis, bit! bimus, bitis, bunt!
  a, ae, ae, am, ā! ae, ārum, īs, ās, īs!
  us, ī, ō, um, ō! ī, ōrum, īs, ōs, īs!
  um, ī, ō, um, ō! a, ōrum, īs, a, īs!
  sum, es, est! sumus, estis, sunt!
  eram, erās, erat! erāmus, erātis, erant!
  erō, eris, erit! erimus, eritis, erunt!

D. Write the four principal parts of the following verbs. Then chant each verb "set" ten times through.

  convocō
  errō
  explorō
  prohibeō
  terreō

E. Decline:

peritus discipulus

primum exemplum

Challenge:

parva avis (Hint: avis is an i-stem noun)

F. Translate the following review sentences.

1. Filiōs vīdistī.

2. Nautās vīdī.

3. Bonum vīnum habuī.

4. Agricola et fēmina parva gladiōs habuērunt.

5. Parvae Puellae fēminās amāvērunt.

6. Laudāverant.

7. Laudāte!

8. Malum cōnsilium malus agricola laudāvit.

9. Parvum dōnum laudābant.

10. Magnum Deum amāmus.

G. Translate the following English into Latin.

1. She saw the king with the troops.

2. The faithful sons had seen the mountains from the window of the farmhouse.

3. The king's son will have warned the scout about the swamp.

4. The evil king saw the great fire from the mountain.

5. God will warn the small son of the father and mother.

6. The king's grandson walked to the mountain with the old man.

7. The young woman will have pleased the guest with flowers.

8. The farmer's strength kept back the cattle.

9. The woman's faithful slaves had pleased the mother of the girl.

10. The bad slaves of the good father walked from the town.

H. Translate the following Latin into English.
1. Vīdī lūcem.

2. Patrēs prohibuit.

3. Mātrēs ignem habuērunt.

4. Pater vīnum laudāverat.

5. Rēx fīlium fēminae vīderit.

6. Servus lēgēs laudat.

7. Servus rēgem videt.

8. Vīdistis montēs.

9. Servus mātrēs prohibuerit.

10. Servī rēgem vīderint.

11. Mercātor lapidem pulchrum magnī aedificiī rēgis laudāvit.

12. Pastor vallum longum flōribus complevit.

13. Rēx leōnēs ferōs in silvā prope turrim virgōnis habēbat.

14. Lūx pastōrī laetō magnam saepe inter silvam et turrim dēmōnstrāvit.

15. Juvenis virginem trepidam per tempestātem horrendam appropinquāvit.

I. Give a synopsis of the following verbs.

1. *videō*—third person, plural

2. *laudō*—second person, singular

3. *ambulō*—first person, plural

4. *portō*—third person, singular

5. *dō*—second person, plural

6. *habeō*—first person, singular

J. List all the English words you can think of which come from this lesson's vocabulary words.

1.	6.
2.	7.
3.	8.
4.	9.
5.	10.

K. Answer the following questions.

    1. What is the ablative plural form of *gladius*?

    2. How many conjugations are there?

    3. What is the nominative plural ending for the Second Declension?

    4. What cases does *sub* take?

    5. List several uses of the ablative case.

    6. What is the third principal part for the verb *ambulō*?

    7. What is the ablative plural ending for the Third Declension?

    8. What is the accusative singular ending for the Third Declension?

    9. What is the accusative singular form of the word *māter*?

    10. What is the dative plural form of the word *mōns*?

THIRD DECLENSION NEUTER

Third Declension neuter nouns are very similar in their endings to Third Declension masculine and feminine nouns. They differ, however, in two areas.

The first is that, in common with all neuter nouns, the nominative and accusative case endings are the same. The second is that the nominative plural ends with an -*a*.

The following word *tempus* (meaning *time*) is a Third Declension neuter noun, declined according to this pattern. (The places where there is a Third Declension distinction are in italics.)

	SINGULAR	PLURAL
NOMINATIVE	*tempus*	*tempora*
GENITIVE	temporis	temporum
DATIVE	temporī	temporibus
ACCUSATIVE	*tempus*	*tempora*
ABLATIVE	tempore	temporibus

Probably the easiest way to remember these case endings is through memorization for the masculine and feminine endings (*is, is, ī, em, e! es, um, ibus, es, ibus!*), and memorization of the places where the neuter nouns differ (nominative and accusative).

THIRD DECLENSION NEUTER I-STEMS

There are a few Third Declension Neuter I-stem nouns. These nouns end in -*al* or -*e* in the nominative singular. These nouns have -*ī* in the ablative singular as well as an -*i* before the plural endings in the nominative, genitive, and accusative cases. The paradigm looks like this:

	SINGULAR	PLURAL
NOMINATIVE	animal	animal*ia*
GENITIVE	animal*is*	animal*ium*
DATIVE	animal*ī*	animal*ibus*
ACCUSATIVE	animal	animal*ia*
ABLATIVE	animal*ī*	animal*ibus*

VOCABULARY

animal, animalis*, n.	animal
carmen, carminis, n.	song, chang, poem; prophecy
culmen, culminis, n.	top, peak, high point
flumen, fluminis, n.	river
iter, itineris*, n.	journey, trek; route
lītus, lītoris, n.	shore, shoreline
mare, maris*, n.	sea
onus, oneris, , n.	weight, burden
ōs, ōris, n.	mouth, opening
tempus, temporis, , n.	time

* = i-stem noun

EXERCISE NINETEEN

A. Spell out in English how each Latin word should be pronounced and place the accent properly.

    1. mātribus

    2. lūx

    3. pater

    4. mātrem

    5. rēgis

    6. lēgis

    7. lēgēs

    8. patrēs

    9. mātribus

    10. temporis

B. Chant each of the following paradigms ten times through.

    is, is, ī, em, e! ēs, um, ibus, ēs, ibus!
    ī, istī, it! imus, istis, ērunt!
    eram, erās, erat! erāmus, erātis, erant!
    erō, eris, erit! erimus, eritis, erint!

C. Chant each of the following paradigms two times through.

    ō, s, t! mus, tis, nt!
    bam, bās, bat! bāmus, bātis, bant!
    bō, bis, bit! bimus, bitis, bunt!
    a, ae, ae, am, ā! ae, ārum, īs, ās, īs!
    us, ī, ō, um, ō! ī, ōrum, īs, ōs, īs!
    um, ī, ō, um, ō! a, ōrum, īs, a, īs!
    sum, es, est! sumus, estis, sunt!
    eram, erās, erat! erāmus, erātis, erant!
    erō, eris, erit! erimus, eritis, erunt!

D. Write the four principal parts of the following verbs. Then chant each verb "set" ten times through.

    habitō

    laborō

    laudō

    videō

    caleō

E. Decline:

parvum antrum

flōs novus

lītus pulchrum

Challenge:

iter asperum (Hint: iter is an i-stem noun)

F. Translate the following review sentences.
1. Montem vīdistī.

2. Montēs vīdī.

3. Ignem bonum habuī.

4. Fēmina parva ignem habet.

5. Puellae parvae matrēs laudāvērunt.

6. Laudāverint.

7. Portā!

8. Noctem agricola malus vīdit.

9. Dōnum parvum spectābant.

10. Deum magnum amant.

G. Translate the following English into Latin.
1. The tired king saw the fire from the distant hill.

2. The faithful son had seen the sheep.

3. The journey will have pleased the son of the king.

4. The grateful people praised the just laws.

5. God will warn the son of the faithful father.

6. Time praised the king's son.

7. The woman's happy son walked into the quiet night.

8. The king loved the laws of God.

9. Do the songs of children please good mothers?

10. The Law of God does not have bad laws.

H. Translate the following Latin into English.
   1. Ad rēgem gladium portō.

   2. Lītus flumen ab urbe prohibuit.

   3. Māter ignem habet.

   4. Pater vīnum prohibuit.

   5. Rēx fīlium mātris vīderit.

   6. Lēx Deī famulum laudat.

   7. Lēx Deī bonum rēgem placuerat.

   8. Montem vīdistī.

   9. Servī animalia prohibuerant.

   10. Servī rēgem vidēbant.

I. Give a synopsis of the following verbs.

    1. *videō*—first person, plural

    2. *laudō*—third person, singular

    3. *ambulō*—second person, plural

    4. *portō*—first person, singular

    5. *dō*—third person, plural

    6. *habeō*—second person, singular

J. List all the English words you can think of which come from this lesson's vocabulary words.

1.   6.

2.   7.

3.   8.

4.   9.

5.   10.

K. Answer the following questions.

1. What is the ablative plural form of *ignis*?

2. How many declensions are there?

3. What is the nominative singular ending for the Second Declension?

4. What case does *post* take?

5. List two uses of the ablative case.

6. What is the third principal part for the verb *habeō*?

7. What is the ablative singular ending for the Third Declension Neuter?

8. What two cases are the same in the Third Declension Neuter?

9. What is the accusative plural form of the word *tempus*?

10. What is the dative singular form of the word *mōns*?

THIRD DECLENSION ADJECTIVES

You have already learned that an adjective must match the noun it modifies in *gender*, *number*, and *case*. But it does not have to match the noun it modifies in *declension*. For example, the adjectives you have learned thus far follow the pattern of First and Second Declension nouns. But what if one of these adjectives (say, *bonus*) is used to modify a Third Declension noun (say, *māter*)?

The adjective must match in gender, number and case but the case endings will not *look* the same. The combination would look like this—*bona māter*.

It is important to emphasize this point here because we have now come to the point where we will learn some adjectives which follow the Third Declension in their case endings. When they are used to modify First or Second Declension nouns, the same things applies. They are to match in gender, number, and case.

VOCABULARY

ācer, ācris, ācre	sharp, fierce
brevis, breve	short, brief
celer, celeris, celere	swift, speedy
facilis, facile	easy
fortis, forte	brave, strong
gravis, grave	serious, grave; heavy
omnis, omne	all, every
similis, simile	like, similar
lātus, -a, -um	broad, wide
līber, lībera, līberum	free (Children were free persons, but not yet citizens in the Roman household. From this situation comes the noun *līberī*, meaning *children*.)
meus, -a, -um	my, mine (In Latin the possessive adjective is omitted except for emphasis or clarification.)
multus, -a, -um	much, (pl.) many
tuus, -a, -um	your, yours (belonging to one person)

You should notice that some of these adjectives are listed in two forms, and some in three. The reason for this is very simple. An adjective must be able to come in three genders—masculine, feminine, and neuter—because it has to be able to match a noun of any gender.

When Third Declension adjectives are listed in two forms, this means that the first form covers both the masculine and the feminine, while the second form is neuter. To take an example from above, *facilis* has all the same case endings whether the noun it modifies is masculine or feminine. If the noun is neuter, then *facile* is what you use.

When three forms are listed, the first is masculine, the second feminine, and the third neuter—just like with *bonus*, *-a*, *-um*. But even here the difference is not as great as it first appears. The only place the masculine and feminine differ is in the nominative singular ending. The rest of the case endings agree. Like neuter i-stem nouns, third declension adjectives end in *-ī* in the ablative singular and in *-ium* in the genitive plural.

In the paradigm below, there are three columns. But note the agreement between the masculine and feminine columns.

	MASCULINE	FEMININE	NEUTER
SINGULAR			
NOMINATIVE	fortis	fortis	forte
GENITIVE	fortis	fortis	fortis
DATIVE	fortī	fortī	fortī
ACCUSATIVE	fortem	fortem	forte
ABLATIVE	*fortī*	*fortī*	*fortī*
PLURAL			
NOMINATIVE	fortēs	fortēs	fortia
GENITIVE	*fortium*	*fortium*	*fortium*
DATIVE	fortibus	fortibus	fortibus
ACCUSATIVE	fortēs	fortēs	fortia
ABLATIVE	fortibus	fortibus	fortibus

EXERCISE TWENTY

A. Spell out in English how each Latin word should be pronounced and place the accent properly.

1. facilibus
2. fortī
3. gravis
4. similīs
5. similem
6. omnēs
7. breve
8. ācribus
9. ācre
10. forte

B Chant each of the following paradigms ten times through.

is, is, ī, em, e! ēs, um, ibus, ēs, ibus!

ī, istī, it! imus, istis, ērunt!

eram, erās, erat! erāmus, erātis, erant!

erō, eris, erit! erimus, eritis, erint!

C. Chant each of the following paradigms two times through.

> ō, s, t! mus, tis, nt!
> bam, bās, bat! bāmus, bātis, bant!
> bō, bis, bit! bimus, bitis, bunt!
> a, ae, ae, am, ā! ae, ārum, īs, ās, īs!
> us, ī, ō, um, ō! ī, ōrum, īs, ōs, īs!
> um, ī, ō, um, ō! a, ōrum, īs, a, īs!
> sum, es, est! sumus, estis, sunt!
> eram, erās, erat! erāmus, erātis, erant!
> erō, eris, erit! erimus, eritis, erunt!

D. Write the four principal parts of the following verbs. Then chant each verb "set" ten times through.

mandō

mutō

narrō

compleō

habeō

E. Decline:

īnsula mea

lūx clara

rēx fortis

Challenge:

gaudium breve

F. Translate the following review sentences.

1. Puellās spectābāmus.

2. Puellam laudābant.

3. Poēta et agricola Deum laudābant.

4. Agricola puellam spectat.

5. Agricolae nōn sumus.

6. Nauta nōn est.

7. Portāte!

8. Fēminae et puellae vocāvērunt.

9. Dōnum magnum spectābant.

10. Christus Deus est.

G. Translate the following English into Latin.
1. The brave king saw the fire.

2. The brave son had seen the night.

3. The mother will have warned the strong son of the serious king.

4. The grave king praised all just laws.

5. God will warn all sons of faithful fathers.

6. The dog has frightened the swift son.

7. The woman's brave son walked into the fierce night.

8. All kings do not love the laws of God.

9. The law of God does not praise fierce sailors.

10. The law of God does not praise all girls.

H. Translate the following Latin into English.
1. Ad rēgem fortem gladium portō.

2. Tempus vocāvit.

3. Māter gravis ignem habet.

4. Pater vīnum similem laudāvit.

5. Rēgēs omnēs fīlium mātris vīderint.

6. Lēx Deī servum brevem laudat.

7. Lēx Deī rēgem fortem laudāverat.

8. Montem omnem vīdistī.

9. Servī fortēs mātrem prohibuerant.

10. Servī rēgem fortem vidēbant.

I. Give a synopsis of the following verbs.
   1. *vocō*—first person, plural

   2. *moneō*—third person, singular

   3. *prohibeō*—second person, plural

   4. *vocō*—first person, singular

5. *moneō*—third person, plural

6. *prohibeō*—second person, singular

J. List all the English words you can think of which come from this lesson's vocabulary words.

1.	6.
2.	7.
3.	8.
4.	9.
5.	10.

K. Answer the following questions.

1. What is the ablative plural form of *vīnum*?

2. How many conjugations are there?

3. What is nominative plural ending for the First Declension?

4. In what things must an adjective match a noun it modifies?

5. List three uses of the ablative case.

6. What is the third principal part for the verb *moneō*?

7. What is the accusative singular ending for a Third Declension Neuter adjective?

8. What is the dative singular ending for a Third Declension masculine adjective?

9. What is the accusative plural masculine form of the word *gravis*?

10. What is the dative singular feminine form of the word *celer*?

READING THREE

This reading is just for fun! If you are artistic, you may wish to draw a picture depicting your understanding of the story.

VIR, LEO, ET SAGITTA

Vir in collēs cum arcū vēnit. Omnia animālia praeter leōnem cucurrērunt. Leō pugnāre mansit. Sed vir leōnem sagittā ferīvit et dīxit, "Sagitta meus nūntius est. Cognōsce nūntium, tum veniam."

Leō currere incēpit, sed vulpes dīxit, "Es fortis. Manē."

Leō respondit, "Numquam mihi persuadēbis. Nūntius virī horrendus est. Virum nōn convenīre cupiō."

Morum praecepta (moral): Verbum unum ad sapientem satis est.

VOCABULARY

arcus, -ūs, m.	bow
currō, currere, cucurrī, cursum	to run, hasten
feriō, -īre, -īvī, -ītum	to smite, strike
maneō, -ēre, mānsī, mānsum	stay, remain
mihi (personal pronoun dative case)	me
numquam	(adv.) never
persuadeō, -ēre, -suāsī, -suāsum	(used with dative) to persuade
praeter	(prep. with accusative) except
pugnō, -āre, āvī, ātum	to fight
respondeō, -ēre, -spondī, responsum	to answer, respond
sagitta, -ae, f.	arrow
satis	(adv.) enough
sīc	(adv.) so, to such a degree
vulpes, -is, f.	fox

THIRD CONJUGATION VERBS: ALL SIX TENSES

The formation of the various verb tenses should be somewhat familiar by now. So as we come to the Third Conjugation, we will learn all six tenses at once.

Third Conjugation verbs are identified by their second principal part. If it ends in -*ere* it belongs to the Third Conjugation. Be careful! The Second Conjugation looks as though it ends in -*ere*, but it actually ends in -*ēre*. For example, *vidēre* looks like a possible Third Conjugation contender. But its present stem is formed by dropped the -*re* from the second principal part *videō*. This gives us a present stem of *vidē*, and that means the ending in the second principal part is simply -*re*.

In the Third Conjugation, if the -*ō* of the first principal part is dropped, this forms the present stem. If the -*ī* is dropped from the third principal part, this forms the perfect stem. The Third Conjugation differs from the first two conjugations in three basic ways.

The first difference is seen in the present tense. The endings are the same (*ō, s, t, mus, tis, nt*), but if these endings were added to the stem of the verb, pronounciation would be difficult. So, between most of the endings and the stem an *i* or a *u* is added. We will demonstrate with the Third Conjugation verb for *rule—regō, regere, rēxī, rēctum*. In the paradigm below, the inserted vowel is italicized. Thus:

	SINGULAR	PLURAL
FIRST PERSON	regō	reg*i*mus
SECOND PERSON	reg*i*s	reg*i*tis
THIRD PERSON	reg*i*t	reg*u*nt

The second difference is found in the imperfect tense. Instead of the letters -*bā* at the beginning of each ending there are the letters -*ēbā*. So between the stem and the endings you have already memorized (*bam, bās, bat, bāmus, bātis, bant*) insert an *ē*.

	SINGULAR	PLURAL
FIRST PERSON	reg*ē*bam	reg*ē*bāmus
SECOND PERSON	reg*ē*bās	reg*ē*bātis
THIRD PERSON	reg*ē*bat	reg*ē*bant

The third difference is in the future tense. Instead of the familiar *bō, bis, bit* endings the indication of the future is an -*ē*-, which becomes an -*a*- in the first person singular, and which is a short -*e*- in both third person singular and plural. The endings are *m, s, t, mus, tis, nt*—the same as the present tense except for the first person singular.

	SINGULAR	PLURAL
FIRST PERSON	reg*a*m	reg*ē*mus
SECOND PERSON	reg*ē*s	reg*ē*tis
THIRD PERSON	reg*e*t	regent

The three tenses of the perfect system are formed in exactly the same way as the first two conjugations and with exactly the same endings. First, the perfect stem is *rēx-*, and the endings of *ī, istī, it, imus, istis, ērunt* are added to form the perfect tense:

	SINGULAR	PLURAL
FIRST PERSON	rēxī	rēximus
SECOND PERSON	rēxistī	rēxistis
THIRD PERSON	rēxit	rēxērunt

With the pluperfect, the same stem is used (*rēx-*), and the endings of *eram, erās, erat, erāmus, erātis, erant* are added.

	SINGULAR	PLURAL
FIRST PERSON	rēxeram	rēxerāmus
SECOND PERSON	rēxerās	rēxerātis
THIRD PERSON	rēxerat	rēxerant

And with the future perfect, it is just the same. *Erō, eris, erit, erimus, eritis, erint* are added to *rēx-*.

	SINGULAR	PLURAL
FIRST PERSON	rēxerō	rēxerimus
SECOND PERSON	rēxeris	rēxeritis
THIRD PERSON	rēxerit	rēxerint

VOCABULARY

Below are listed some Third Conjugation verbs.

cognōscō, cognōscere, cognōvī, cognitum	recognize
dēfendō, dēfendere, dēfendī, dēfēnsum	defend
dīcō, dicere, dīxī, dictum	tell, say
dūcō, dūcere, dūxī, ductum	lead, guide
mittō, mittere, mīsī, missum	send
pōnō, pōnere, posuī, positum	put, place
regō, regere, rēxī, rēctum	rule
relinquō, relinquere, relīquī, relictum	leave behind
surgō, surgere, surrēxī, surrēctum	rise
vincō, vincere, vīcī, victum	defeat, conquer

EXERCISE TWENTY-ONE

A. Spell out in English how each Latin word should be pronounced and place the accent properly.

1. regēbāmus

2. regēbant

3. regēbātis

4. regit

5. regunt

6. regimus

7. rēxī

8. rēxērunt

9. rēxerit

10. rēxerimus

B. Chant each of the following paradigms ten times through.

ō, s, t! mus, tis, nt!

bam, bās, bat! bāmus, bātis, bant!

bō, bis, bit! bimus, bitis, bunt!

a, ae, ae, am, ā! ae, ārum, īs, ās, īs!

us, ī, ō, um, ō! ī, ōrum, īs, ōs, īs!

um, ī, ō, um, ō! a, ōrum, īs, a, īs!

sum, es, est! sumus, estis, sunt!

eram, erās, erat! erāmus, erātis, erant!

erō, eris, erit! erimus, eritis, erunt!

ī, istī, it! imus, istis, ērunt!

eram, erās, erat! erāmus, erātis, erant!

erō, eris, erit! erimus, eritis, erint!

is, is, ī, em, e! ēs, um, ibus, ēs, ibus!

C. Write the four principal parts of the following verbs. Then chant each verb "set" ten times through.

navigō

iaceō

dēfendō

dīcō

dūcō

D. Decline:

magnus agricola

leō fortis

Challenge:

mare ācre

E. Translate the following review sentences.

1. Puellam spectābāmus.

2. Puellās et nautam laudābant.

3. Poēta et fēminae Deum laudābant.

4. Agricolae puellās spectant.

5. Fēminae nōn sumus.

6. Agricola nōn est.

7. Ambulāte!

8. Fēminae puellam vocāvērunt.

9. Dōnum magnum spectābunt.

10. Christus Fīlius Deī est.

F. Translate the following English into Latin.

1. The brave king will lead the legions.

2. The brave son had recognized the king.

3. The mothers told the sons of the evil king about the danger.

4. The Son of God ruled the grave king.

5. God will defeat all evil sons of evil mothers.

6. The swift son will leave the women behind.

7. The woman's son sent the scout into town.

8. Evil kings did not recognize the laws of God.

9. The Law of God will not defend evil sons.

10. The laws of God do not rule all women.

G. Translate the following Latin into English.
   1. Rēgem fortem vincimus.

   2. Rēx rēxit.

   3. Māter gravis fīlium relinquit.

   4. Pater vīnum pōnit.

   5. Rēx oppidum dēfenderit.

   6. Lēx Deī bonum fīlium dūxit.

   7. Lēx Deī rēgem vincit.

   8. Cognōvērunt montem omnem.

   9. Māter servōs mīserat.

   10. Servī surrēxerint.

H. Give a synopsis of the following verbs.
   1. dīcō—first person, plural

2. cognōscō—third person, singular

3. vincō—second person, plural

4. surgō—first person, singular

5. relinquō—third person, plural

6. regō—second person, singular

I. List all the English words you can think of which come from this lesson's vocabulary words.

1.	6.
2.	7.
3.	8.
4.	9.
5.	10.

J. Answer the following questions.

1. What are the case endings for the First Declension?

2. What are the case endings for the Second Declension?

3. What are the case endings for the Third Declension?

4. What are the case endings for the Second Declension Neuter?

5. What are the conjugational endings for the imperfect tense, First Conjugation?

6. What is the third principal part for the verb *pōnō*?

7. To which conjugation does *dūcō* belong?

8. To which conjugation does *ambulō* belong?

9. To which conjugation does *mittō* belong?

10. What is the second principal part for the verb *surgō*?

THIRD CONJUGATION: I-STEM VERBS

There is an important variant of the Third Conjugation. Verbs that follow this pattern are called *i-stem* verbs. Like other Third Conjugation verbs, the second principal part ends in *-ere*. But unlike other Third Conjugation verbs, *io* verbs contain an extra *i* that sets them apart.

Take, for example, the verb that means make or do—*faciō, facere, fēcī, factum*. The *-ere* on the end of *facere* tells us that it is a Third Conjugation. And when we go to form the present stem by dropping the *o* from the first principal part, we see that the stem is *faci*—clearly an i-stem.

Given this difference in the stem, the conjugation is formed just like normal Third Declension verbs. Let's start with the present tense, and go through our normal order of tenses:

	SINGULAR	PLURAL
PRESENT		
FIRST PERSON	capiō	capimus
SECOND PERSON	capis	capitis
THIRD PERSON	capit	capiunt
IMPERFECT		
FIRST PERSON	capiēbam	capiēbāmus
SECOND PERSON	capiēbās	capiēbātis
THIRD PERSON	capiēbat	capiēbant
FUTURE		
FIRST PERSON	capiam	capiēmus
SECOND PERSON	capiēs	capiētis
THIRD PERSON	capiet	capient
PERFECT		
FIRST PERSON	cēpī	cēpimus
SECOND PERSON	cēpistī	cēpistis
THIRD PERSON	cēpit	cēpērunt
PLUPERFECT		
FIRST PERSON	cēperam	cēperāmus
SECOND PERSON	cēperās	cēperātis
THIRD PERSON	cēperat	cēperant
FUTURE PERFECT		
FIRST PERSON	cēperō	cēperimus
SECOND PERSON	cēperis	cēperitis
THIRD PERSON	cēperit	cēperint

Vocabulary

accipiō, accipere, accēpī, acceptum	accept, receive
capiō, capere, cēpī, captum	take, seize, capture
cōnficiō, cōnficere, cōnfēcī, cōnfectum	finish
cupiō, cupere, cupīvī, cupītum	desire, wish, want
faciō, facere, fēcī, factum	make, do
incipiō, incipere, incēpī, inceptum	begin
interficiō, interficere, interfēcī, interfectum	kill

Exercise Twenty-Two

A. Spell out in English how each Latin word should be pronounced and place the accent properly.

1. faciēmus

2. faciam

3. facit

4. faciunt

5. fēcistī

6. fēcerimus

7. fēcī

8. cōnficere

9. cōnfectum

10. cupīvī

B. Chant each of the following paradigms five times through.

ō, s, t! mus, tis, nt!
bam, bās, bat! bāmus, bātis, bant!
bō, bis, bit! bimus, bitis, bunt!
a, ae, ae, am, ā! ae, ārum, īs, ās, īs!
us, ī, ō, um, ō! ī, ōrum, īs, ōs, īs!
um, ī, ō, um, ō! a, ōrum, īs, a, īs!
sum, es, est! sumus, estis, sunt!
eram, erās, erat! erāmus, erātis, erant!
erō, eris, erit! erimus, eritis, erunt!
ī, istī, it! imus, istis, ērunt!
eram, erās, erat! erāmus, erātis, erant!
erō, eris, erit! erimus, eritis, erint!
is, is, ī, em, e! ēs, um, ibus, ēs, ibus!

C. Write the four principal parts of the following verbs. Then chant each verb "set" ten times through.

oppugnō

impendō

cognōscō

mittō

accipiō

D. Decline:

parvum antrum

flōs novus

Challenge:

lītus breve

E. Translate the following review sentences.

1. Agricolae nōn sumus.

2. Dōnum est.

3. Fēminae Deum laudābant.

4. Deus Fīlium dabat.

5. Poētae cōnsilium dant.

6. Nauta et puella fēminam amābant.

7. Laudāte!

8. Amāveratne Deus mundum?

9. Nōnne dederat cōnsilium?

10. Vocāverintne fēminae et puellae?

F. Translate the following English into Latin.

1. The brave king accepts the gift.

2. The brave sons didn't kill the king, did they?

3. Did the mother receive the sons of the evil king?

4. The grave king will finish the plan.

5. He desires to have a sword.

6. The women begin to shout.

7. They killed all the men in the evil city.

8. Evil kings did not receive the laws of God.

9. We do not always want the law of God.

10. The king accepted the gift of the faithful sons.

G. Translate the following Latin into English.

1. Rēgem fortem interficit.

2. Cōnsilium fēcī.

3. Māter gravis cōnsilium accipit.

4. Pater vīnum accēpit.

5. Fīliōs fortēs habēre cupīvit.

6. Incipiō.

7. Incēpimus.

8. Confēcerat.

9. Māter servōs accēpit.

10. Servī interfēcērunt.

H. The following sentences give the Roman explanation of how man became acquainted with fire. Translate them into English.

1. Prométheus (a Roman god) incolās terrae fēcit.

2. Incolae in antrīs obscūrīs et in villīs gelidīs habitāvērunt.

3. Prométheus incolās amāvit et dīxit, "Ignem ad incolās terrae dē Olympō cupiō portāre."

4. Nocte obscūrā Prométheus ignem cēpit et ignem cum incolīs terrae posuit.

5. Incolae terrae bonum dōnum magnō cum gaudiō accēpērunt et mox multae flammae clārae in terrā calēbant.

I. Give a synopsis of the following verbs.

1. *faciō*—first person, plural

2. *accipiō*—third person, singular

3. *interficiō*—second person, plural

4. *incipiō*—first person, singular

5. *cupiō*—third person, plural

6. *cōnficiō*—second person, singular

J. List all the English words you can think of which come from this lesson's vocabulary words.

1.	6.
2.	7.
3.	8.
4.	9.
5.	10.

K. Answer the following questions.

1. What are the conjugational endings for the present tense, First Conjugation?

2. What are the conjugational endings for the future tense, Second Conjugation?

3. What are the conjugational endings for the future tense, Third Conjugation?

4. What is the dative plural ending for the Fourth Declension?

5. What is the genitive singular ending for the Second Declension?

6. What is the third principal part for the verb *interficiō*?

7. To which conjugation does *vincō* belong?

8. To which conjugation does *mittō* belong?

9. To which conjugation does *dēfendō* belong?

10. What is the second principal part for the verb *ambulō*?

READING FOUR

This reading is a commonly known story. It may interest you to know that the Bible is written in advanced Latin, even in passages that are simple to understand. Many of the verbs in this selection were changed from subjunctive mood which you will learn later to the imperative mood which you already know.

GENESIS 1:1-10

In principiō creāvit Deus caelum et terram. Terra autem erat inānis et vacua, et tenebrae erant super faciem abyssī, et Spiritus Dei [movēbat] super aquās. Dīxitque Deus: Es lūx. Et [erat] lūx. Et vīdit Deus lūcem. [Lūx erat] bona: et dīvīsit lūcem ā tenebrīs. Appellāvit lūcem Diem, et tenebrās Noctem: [et erat] vespere et māne, diēs unus. Dīxit quoque Deus: [Es] firmāmentum in mediō aquārum: et dīvīde aquās ab aquīs. Et fēcit Deus firmāmentum, dīvīsitque aquās, quae erant sub firmāmentō, ab hīs, quae erant super firmāmentum. Et [erat] ita. Vocāvitque Deus firmāmentum, Caelum: et [erat] vespere et māne, diēs secundus. Dīxit vērō Deus: [Congregāte] aquae, quae sub caelō sunt, in locum unum: et [apparē] arida. Et [erat] ita. Et vocāvit Deus aridam Terram, congregātiōnēsque aquārum appellāvit Maria. Et vīdit Deus [omnia]. [Omnia erat] bona.

VOCABULARY

abyssī	(Second Decl., gen.) of the deep, depths, abyss
appāreō,-ēre, -uī, -itum	to appear, to begin to be visible
appellō, -āre, -āvī, -ātum	to name, to call
aqua, -ae, f.	water
aridus, -a, -um	(adj.) dry, (here: dry land)
congregātiō, congregātiōnis, f.	an assembling together, society, union
faciem (from faciēs)	face
firmāmentum -ī, n. (from *firmō*)	a support, prop
inānis, ināne	(adj.) without form, void
ita	(adv.) thus, like this
principium, -ī, n.,	beginning
quae (relative pronoun)	which
quoque	and, and also
-que (enclitic ending)	and
sub	under
super	(adv.) over, above
vacuus, -a, -um	(adj.) empty, vacant

QUESTIONS:

1. Quī (who) terram fēcit?

2. Ubi Spiritus Deī erat?

3. Ubi firmamentum posuit?

4. Quid (what) Deus congregātiōnēs aquārum appellāvit?

GRAMMAR EXERCISE:

Choose a sentence from the story. Label each noun or adjective with its *gender, number,* and *case,* and each verb with its *person, number,* and *tense.* Then decline all the nouns in your sentence and do a synopsis of all the verbs.

FOURTH DECLENSION

The nominative singular for the Fourth Declension is the same as the nominative singular of the Second Declension—*us*. It is therefore important to determine which declension a -*us* noun is in when you learn it. You should recall that this is done by looking at the genitive singular, which will always be listed in the dictionary or word list.

A Second Declension noun will be listed this way:

Deus,-ī, m.—God

A Fourth Declension noun will be listed this way:

impetus, impetūs, m.—attack

The genitive singular of Second Declension nouns is -*ī*, while the genitive singular ending of Fourth Declension Masculine and Feminine nouns is -*ūs*. The case endings for masculine and feminine nouns of the Fourth Declension look like this:

	SINGULAR	PLURAL
NOMINATIVE	man*us*	man*ūs*
GENITIVE	man*ūs*	man*uum*
DATIVE	man*uī*	man*ibus*
ACCUSATIVE	man*um*	man*ūs*
ABLATIVE	man*ū*	man*ibus*

VOCABULARY

Here is a list of Fourth Declension nouns. You will notice that most of them are masculine. Except for *domus, manus,* and the names of trees, which are feminine, most Fourth Declension nouns ending in -*us* in the nominative are masculine in gender. Nouns ending in -*ū* in the nominative are neuter nouns.

adventus, adventūs, m.	approach, arrival
casus, casūs, m.	misfortune
cursus, -ūs, m.	running; course
domus, domūs, f.	home, house (This noun has some irregularities. The ablative singular is *domō*, and the accusative plural is *domōs*.)
exercitus, -ūs, m.	army
exitus, exitūs, m.	departure
fluctus, -ūs, m.	wave (of the sea)
impetus, impetūs, m.	attack
manus, manūs, f.	hand; band of men
occāsus, -ūs, m.	setting, a going down
sōlis occāsus	sunset, sundown
portus, -ūs, m.	harbor, port

FOURTH DECLENSION NEUTER

cornū, cornūs, n.   horn; (*in military literature*: wing of an army)

	SINGULAR	PLURAL
NOMINATIVE	corn*ū*	corn*ua*
GENITIVE	corn*ūs*	corn*uum*
DATIVE	corn*ū*	corn*ibus*
ACCUSATIVE	corn*ū*	corn*ua*
ABLATIVE	corn*ū*	corn*ibus*

Notice the common feature of neuter nouns—the nominative and accusative, both singular and plural, match.

EXERCISE TWENTY-THREE

A. Spell out in English how each Latin word should be pronounced and place the accent properly.

1. manūs

2. manibus

3. manū

4. adventum

5. adventibus

6. adventuī

7. manuum

8. casuum

9. exitibus

10. impetibus

B. Chant each of the following paradigms five times through, beginning at the bottom and chanting you way to the top!

ō, s, t! mus, tis, nt!
bam, bās, bat! bāmus, bātis, bant!
bō, bis, bit! bimus, bitis, bunt!
a, ae, ae, am, ā! ae, ārum, īs, ās, īs!
us, ī, ō, um, ō! ī, ōrum, īs, ōs, īs!
um, ī, ō, um, ō! a, ōrum, īs, a, īs!
sum, es, est! sumus, estis, sunt!
eram, erās, erat! erāmus, erātis, erant!
erō, eris, erit! erimus, eritis, erunt!

ī, istī, it! imus, istis, ērunt!
eram, erās, erat! erāmus, erātis, erant!
erō, eris, erit! erimus, eritis, erint!
is, is, ī, em, e! ēs, um, ibus, ēs, ibus!
us, ūs, uī, um, ū! ūs, uum, ibus, ūs, ibus!

C. Write the four principal parts of the following verbs. Then chant each verb "set" ten times through.

portō

moneō

maneō

dēfendō

capiō

D. Decline:

līberī meī

omnis bōs

coniunx similis

Challenge:

adulēscēns celer

E. Translate the following review sentences.

1. Agricolae et nautae nōn sumus.

2. Dōnum bonum est.

3. Fēmina Deum laudābit.

4. Deus Fīlium dedit.

5. Poēta cōnsilium bonum dat.

6. Nautae et puellae fēminās amābunt.

7. Spectāte!

8. Amāverantne mundum?

9. Nōnne dederant cōnsilium malum?

10. Spectāverintne fēminae et puellae?

F. Translate the following English into Latin.
1. The brave king praises the attack.

2. The mother does not want misfortune.

3. The woman accepted the arrival of the evil king.

4. The farmer recognized the house.

5. He desires a swift departure.

6. The women saw the arrival of the army.

7. They led the attack.

8. We saw the hand of God.

9. The law of God is not misfortune.

10. The king defended the port of the high city.

G. Translate the following Latin into English.
1. Rēgis fortis impetum laudāvit.

2. Fēminae adventum spectant.

3. Māter gravis domum accipit.

4. Pater manum agricolae accēpit.

5. Casum cupīvit.

6. Impetum cupīvit.

7. Exitum rēgis spectāmus.

8. Rēx impetum laudābit.

9. Māter servōs domūs accēpit.

10. Servī casum spectāvērunt.

H. Give a synopsis of the following verbs.
   1. *faciō*—second person, plural

   2. *accipiō*—first person, singular

   3. *interficiō*—third person, plural

   4. *incipiō*—second person, singular

   5. *cupiō*—first person, plural

6. *cōnficiō*—third person, singular

I. List all the English words you can think of which come from this lesson's vocabulary words.

1.   6.

2.   7.

3.   8.

4.   9.

5.   10.

J. Answer the following questions.

1. How many conjugations are there?

2. How many declensions are there?

3. What is the genitive singular ending for *rēx*?

4. What is the dative plural ending for *agricola*?

5. What is the genitive singular ending for the Second Declension?

6. What are the case endings for the Fourth Declension?

7. What are the case endings for the Fourth Declension Neuter?

8. What is apposition?

9. What is a predicate nominative?

10. What case does the preposition *ad* take?

FOURTH CONJUGATION

We come now to the last of the four conjugations for Latin verbs. You should recall that the second principal part of First Conjugation verbs ends with *-āre*, Second Conjugation with *-ēre*, and Third Conjugation with *-ere*. The second principal part for the Fourth Conjugation ends with *-īre*. They can also be recognized by the fact that the present stem for the verb ends with an *i*.

Here are the four principal parts of a Fourth Conjugation verb:

audiō, audīre, audīvī, audītum—hear

PRESENT

The present stem is found the same way as for the first and second conjugations. Drop the *-re* from the second principal part here, and you have *audī*. This the present stem.

Now we can form the various tenses for this verb.

	SINGULAR	PLURAL
FIRST PERSON	audiō	audīmus
SECOND PERSON	audīs	audītis
THIRD PERSON	audit	audiunt

IMPERFECT

The same thing is done in this tense that is done for the third conjugation. The sign for this tense is an *-ēbā-* between the stem and the ending. In the imperfect and future tenses, the *-ī* of the present stem "yields" its macron to the *-ē* of the tense indicator.

	SINGULAR	PLURAL
FIRST PERSON	audiēbam	audiēbāmus
SECOND PERSON	audiēbās	audiēbātis
THIRD PERSON	audiēbat	audiēbant

FUTURE

The same is true for the future tense. It is formed in the same way as for Third Conjugation verbs.

	SINGULAR	PLURAL
FIRST PERSON	audiam	audiēmus
SECOND PERSON	audiēs	audiētis
THIRD PERSON	audiet	audient

PERFECT

The next three tenses of the perfect system are formed in the same fashion as all other conjugations. The endings are added to the stem of the third principal part.

	SINGULAR	PLURAL
FIRST PERSON	audīvī	audīvimus
SECOND PERSON	audīvistī	audīvistis
THIRD PERSON	audīvit	audīvērunt

PLUPERFECT

FIRST PERSON	audīveram	audīverāmus
SECOND PERSON	audīverās	audīverātis
THIRD PERSON	audīverat	audīverant

FUTURE PERFECT

FIRST PERSON	audīverō	audīverimus
SECOND PERSON	audīveris	audīveritis
THIRD PERSON	audīverit	audīverint

VOCABULARY

audiō, audīre, audīvī, audītum	hear
conveniō, convenīre, convēnī, conventum	assemble
dormiō, dormīre, dormīvī, dormītum	sleep
impediō, impedīre, impedīvī, impedītum	hinder
inveniō, invenīre, invēnī, inventum	come upon, find
perveniō, pervenīre, pervēnī, perventum	arrive
veniō, venīre, vēnī, ventum*	come

EXERCISE TWENTY-FOUR

A. Spell out in English how each Latin word should be pronounced and place the accent properly.

1. audīre

2. invenīre

3. ventum

4. dormiō

5. perveniō

6. dormītum

7. impedīvī

8. pervēnī

9. pervēnit

10. impedīverint

---

* After one conquest, Caesar sent this concise message back to Rome: "Vēnī, vīdī, vīcī." This report will help you to remember the third principal parts of *veniō, videō, and vincō.*

B. Chant each of the following paradigms two times through.

ō, s, t! mus, tis, nt!
bam, bās, bat! bāmus, bātis, bant!
bō, bis, bit! bimus, bitis, bunt!
a, ae, ae, am, ā! ae, ārum, īs, ās, īs!
us, ī, ō, um, ō! ī, ōrum, īs, ōs, ēs!
um, ī, ō, um, ō! a, ōrum, īs, a, īs!
sum, es, est! sumus, estis, sunt!
eram, erās, erat! erāmus, erātis, erant!
erō, eris, erit! erimus, eritis, erunt!
ī, istī, it! imus, istis, ērunt!
eram, erās, erat! erāmus, erātis, erant!
erō, eris, erit! erimus, eritis, erint!

C. Chant each of the following paradigms ten times through.

is, is, ī, em, e! ēs, um, ibus, ēs, ibus!
us, ūs, uī, um, ū! ūs, uum, ibus, ūs, ibus!

D. Write the four principal parts of the following verbs. Then chant each verb "set" ten times through.

audiō

inveniō

veniō

impediō

dormiō

E. Decline:

dux līber

magna laus

arcus tuus

Challenge:

exitus celer

F. Translate the following review sentences.

1. Rēgem fortem interficit.

2. Cōnsilium fēcī.

3. Māter gravis cōnsilium accipit.

4. Pater vīnum accēpit.

5. Fīliōs fortēs habēre cupīvit.

6. Incipiō.

7. Incēpimus.

8. Confēcerat.

9. Māter servōs accēpit.

10. Servī interfēcērunt.

G. Translate the following English into Latin.

1. The short woman hears the law of God.

2. The mother comes upon the easy road.

3. The woman hinders the arrival of the fierce king.

4. The swift farmer arrives.

5. The tired poets sleep.

6. All the women come and see.

7. They heard the fierce attack.

8. Soon they assembled.

9. Then we arrived.

10. The king hindered the attack of the brave sons.

H. Translate the following Latin into English.

    1. Adulēscēns regem audīvit.

    2. Carmen avium audiō.

    3. Canis acer dormit.

    4. Mōns fīlium impedit.

    5. Cum navibus pervenīmus.

    6. Custōs dormīvit.

    7. Prope fontem convenīmus.

    8. Hospes iuvenēs audit.

    9. Dux leōnēs pugnat.

    10. Viam brevem invēnistis.

I. Give a synopsis of the following verbs.

    1. *audiō*—second person, plural

    2. *inveniō*—first person, singular

    3. *veniō*—third person, plural

4. *impediō*—second person, singular

5. *dormiō*—first person, plural

6. *conveniō*—third person, singular

J. List all the English words you can think of which come from this lesson's vocabulary words.

1.	6.
2.	7.
3.	8.
4.	9.
5.	10.

K. Answer the following questions.

1. What are the case endings for the Third Declension?

2. What are the case endings for the Fourth Declension?

3. What is the genitive plural ending for *rēx*?

4. What is the accusative plural ending for *manus*?

5. What is the Second Principal Part of *audiō*?

6. What is the distinctive ending identifying Fourth Conjugation verbs?

7. What is the Second Principal Part of *dormiō*?

8. What case does *ad* take?

9. What case does *prope* take?

10. What is the infinitive of *dormiō*?

FIFTH DECLENSION

We now come to the last of the five declensions. They can be recognized through the genitive singular case ending which is *-eī*. With just several exceptions, Fifth Declensions nouns are all feminine. The exceptions are the word for day, *diēs*, and another word formed from that word meaning noon—*meridiēs*. The case endings look like this:

	SINGULAR	PLURAL
NOMINATIVE	diēs	diēs
GENITIVE	diēī	diērum
DATIVE	diēī	diēbus
ACCUSATIVE	diem	diēs
ABLATIVE	diē	diēbus

VOCABULARY

diēs, -ēī, m.	day
faciēs, -ēī, f.	shape, form, figure; face
rēs, -ēī, f.	thing
spēs, -ēī, f.	hope

EXERCISE TWENTY-FIVE

A. Spell out in English how each Latin word should be pronounced and place the accent properly.

1. diēs
2. diem
3. rēs
4. spēī
5. meridiem
6. diērum
7. diēbus
8. diē
9. rēī
10. rem

B. Chant each of the following paradigms two times through.

    ō, s, t! mus, tis, nt!

    bam, bās, bat! bāmus, bātis, bant!

    bō, bis, bit! bimus, bitis, bunt!

    a, ae, ae, am, ā! ae, ārum, īs, ās, īs!

    us, ī, ō, um, ō! ī, ōrum, īs, ōs, īs!

    um, ī, ō, um, ō! a, ōrum, īs, a, īs!

    sum, es, est! sumus, estis, sunt!

    eram, erās, erat! erāmus, erātis, erant!

    erō, eris, erit! erimus, eritis, erunt!

C. Chant each of the following paradigms ten times through.

    ī, istī, it! imus, istis, ērunt!

    eram, erās, erat! erāmus, erātis, erant!

    erō, eris, erit! erimus, eritis, erint!

    is, is, ī, em, e! ēs, um, ibus, ēs, ibus!

    us, ūs, uī, um, ū! ūs, uum, ibus, ūs, ibus!

    ēs, ēī, ēī, em, ē! ēs, ērum, ēbus, ēs, ēbus!

    rēs, rēī, rēī, rem, rē! rēs, rērum, rēbus, rēs, rēbus!

D. Write the four principal parts of the following verbs. Then chant each verb "set" ten times through.

    laudō

    spectō

    inveniō

    perveniō

    habeō

    videō

E. Decline:

    puella pulchra

    bellum horrendum

    lūx clara

Challenge:

manus gravis

F. Translate the following review sentences.

1. Fēminam audīvit.

2. Fēminās audiō.

3. Deus nōn dormit.

4. Deus puellās audit.

5. Agricolae oppidum inveniunt.

6. Dormīvēruntne puellae?

7. Rēx impetum laudābat.

8. Nautae casum spectant.

9. Puellae et agricolae domum spectābunt.

10. Adventum rēgis spectāmus.

G. Translate the following English into Latin.

1. The woman hears (her) husband.

2. The scout comes upon the lions.

3. The women hinder the arrival of the maiden.

4. The weary farmer arrived with a burden.

5. The grateful poets slept under the roof.

6. The women came and saw the lofty tower.

7. The king heard the attack of the ship.

8. Often they assembled in the thick forest.

9. Soon we arrived at the mouth of the river.

10. The faithful king hinders the attack of the fierce sons.

H. Translate the following Latin into English.
   1. Rēx spem habet.

   2. Rem fēminārum audiō.

   3. Pater dormīvit.

   4. Pater impetum impedīvit.

   5. Dormīvimus.

   6. Diēs pervenit.

   7. Convēnistis.

   8. Rēx famam iuvenis audit.

   9. Fīlius canem audit.

   10. Longam viam invēnistī.

I. Give a synopsis of the following verbs.
   1. *laudō*—second person, plural

3. *inveniō*—third person, plural

4. *perveniō*—second person, singular

5. *habeō*—first person, plural

6. *videō*—third person, singular

J. List all the English words you can think of which come from this lesson's vocabulary words.

1.   6.

2.   7.

3.   8.

4.   9.

5.   10.

K. Answer the following questions.

1. What case is used for the subject of a sentence?

2. What case is used for the direct object of a sentence?

3. What case is used for the indirect object of a sentence?

4. What case is used to show possession?

5. What case is used to show means?

6. What case is used to show accompaniment?

7. What is the accusative plural of *spēs*?

8. What is the dative plural of *rēs*?

9. What are the case endings of the Fifth Declension?

10. What are the case endings of the Fourth Declension?

Demonstratives As Adjectives

A demonstrative (from *dēmonstrō*) adjective shows or points out a person or thing: *this* boy, *that* dog. In Latin, the demonstrative adjective *hic, haec, hoc* means *this, these* and indicates a noun close to the speaker. *Ille, illa, illud* means *that, those* and points out a noun farther away from the speaker. As all adjectives in Latin, a demonstrative adjective agrees with the noun it points out (modifies) in *gender, number*, and *case*.

Putting all this together, each demonstrative has thirty different forms.

The best way to learn these is through chanting them to yourself. After we look at the first paradigm, we will discuss the best order for learning them. We will start with the demonstrative *this/these*. It looks like this:

	MASCULINE	FEMININE	NEUTER
SINGULAR			
NOMINATIVE	hic	haec	hoc
GENITIVE	huius	huius	huius
DATIVE	huic	huic	huic
ACCUSATIVE	hunc	hanc	hoc
ABLATIVE	hōc	hāc	hōc
PLURAL			
NOMINATIVE	hī	hae	haec
GENITIVE	hōrum	hārum	hōrum
DATIVE	hīs	hīs	hīs
ACCUSATIVE	hōs	hās	haec
ABLATIVE	hīs	hīs	hīs

Now the simplest way to memorize this is to start with the all the cases of the singular first, and then proceed to the cases of the plural. For each case, go left to right—masculine, feminine, neuter. Your chanting for the singular should then sound something like this:

    hic, haec, hoc! huius, huius, huius! huic, huic, huic! hunc, hanc, hoc! hōc, hāc, hōc!

Of course the singular means *this*. The plural means *these*. The columns indicating gender and the rows showing the cases work in the same way they do for the nouns.

But because this may appear confusing, let's work through just a few examples. The concept is simple enough—as soon as you get the hang of it.

If we wanted to say *This farmer looks at this girl*, we have to decide what to do with *this farmer*, and what to do with *this girl*.

Because *farmer* is the subject, and because *farmer* is masculine, our word for this must be nominative and it must be masculine. We would therefore say:

    Hic agricola . . .

Now what do we do with *this girl*? Because girl is the direct object in the sentence, and because girl is feminine, the word for this here must be accusative and feminine. We would therefore say:

    . . . hanc puellam

Putting the whole thing together, we say:

Hic *agricola* hanc *puellam spectat.*

Now let's look at an example from the plural. Now we want to say *These girls look at these farmers.* Now *girls* is the subject and must take the nominative. And *farmers* is the direct object and must take the accusative. And so the adjective *these* must match in gender, number, and case. This gives us:

Hae *puellae* hōs *agricolās spectant.*

Here are a few more practice phrases before we go on to the next paradigm. Tell the gender, number, and case of each phrase and give a possible translation for it.

huic fēminae

tēctum hujus aedificiī

haec bella

in hāc villā

hīs verbīs

The next paradigm is for *that/those.*

	MASCULINE	FEMININE	NEUTER
SINGULAR			
NOMINATIVE	ille	illa	illud
GENITIVE	illīus	illīus	illīus
DATIVE	illī	illī	illī
ACCUSATIVE	illum	illam	illud
ABLATIVE	illō	illā	illō
PLURAL			
NOMINATIVE	illī	illae	illa
GENITIVE	illōrum	illārum	illōrum
DATIVE	illīs	illīs	illīs
ACCUSATIVE	illōs	illās	illa
ABLATIVE	illīs	illīs	illīs

Here are a few practice phrases before we go on to the next paradigm. Tell the gender, number, and case of each phrase and give a possible translation for it.

illa famula

illīus populī

ab illō deō

illī virō

ad illōs pastōrēs

Is, ea, id which may mean *this, these / that, those* is a weaker demonstrative adjective because it merely points out, but does not indicate the position of the noun in relation to the speaker. The next paradigm can mean *this/that, these/those*

	MASCULINE	FEMININE	NEUTER
SINGULAR			
NOMINATIVE	is	ea	id
GENITIVE	eius	eius	eius
DATIVE	eī	eī	eī
ACCUSATIVE	eum	eam	id
ABLATIVE	eō	eā	eō
PLURAL			
NOMINATIVE	eī	eae	ea
GENITIVE	eōrum	eārum	eōrum
DATIVE	eīs	eīs	eīs
ACCUSATIVE	eōs	eās	ea
ABLATIVE	eīs	eīs	eīs

Here are a few practice phrases. Tell the gender, number, and case of each phrase and give a possible translation for it.

in eīs villīs

eās puellās

eōrum patrum

ea ora

sub id tectum

EXERCISE TWENTY-SIX

A. Spell out in English how each Latin word should be pronounced and place the accent properly.

1. hōrum
2. hārum
3. haec
4. hōc
5. huius
6. huic
7. illīus
8. illōrum
9. illud
10. illī

B. Chant each of the following paradigms ten times through.

is, is, ī, em, e! ēs, um, ibus, ēs, ibus!
us, ūs, uī, um, ū! ūs, uum, ibus, ūs, ibus!
ēs, ēī, ēī, em, ē! ēs, ērum, ēbus, ēs, ēbus!
hic, haec, hoc! huius, huius, huius! huic, huic, huic! hunc, hanc, hoc! hōc, hāc, hōc!
hī, hae, haec! hōrum, hārum, hōrum! hīs, hīs, hīs! hōs, hās, haec! hīs, hīs, hīs!
ille, illa, illud! illīus, illīus, illīus! illī, illī, illī! illum, illam, illud! illō, illā, illō!
illī, illae, illa! illōrum, illārum, illōrum! illīs, illīs, illīs! illōs, illās, illa! illīs, illīs, illīs!
is, ea, id! eius, eius, eius! eī, eī, eī! eum, eam, id! eō, eā, eō!
eī, eae, ea! eōrum, eārum, eōrum! eīs, eīs, eīs! eōs, eās, ea! eīs, eīs, eīs!

C. Write the four principal parts of the following verbs. Then chant each verb "set" ten times through.

videō
faciō
cupiō
incipiō
interficiō
moneō

D. Decline:

is puer

illa famula

hoc onus

E. Translate the following review sentences.

1. Agricolae et nautae Deum audīvērunt.

2. Dōna bona dant.

3. Fēminae audient.

4. Fīlius pervenit.

5. Fēminae convēnērunt.

6. Puellae fēminās audient.

7. Poēta Deum invenit.

8. Pervēnī.

9. Puellae et agricolae ad oppidum ambulābant.

10. Fēminae et puellae dormīverant.

F. Translate the following English into Latin.

1. This woman hears the law of God.

2. That mother comes upon this road.

3. The woman hinders the arrival of this king.

4. These farmers arrive.

5. These poets sleep, but those poets always labor.

6. Those women come and see.

7. They heard this attack.

8. This king heard that attack.

9. These poets saw that girl.

10. This woman hindered that man.

Use *is, ea, id* for the following translations.
11. This horse is running in the field.

12. That man overcomes the horse.

13. Did you see those swift birds?

14. Why are these tired watchmen standing in the river?

15. Those men have fought a long war.

G. Translate the following Latin into English.
1. Illum rēgem audīvit.

2. Illās fēminās audiō.

3. Haec māter gravis dormit.

4. Hic pater fīlium impedit.

5. Hī poētae illās puellās spectant.

6. Hic agricola dormīvit.

7. Ille rēx Deum laudāvit.

8. Illae fēminae audient.

9. Māter illōs servōs audit.

10. Illam viam invēnistis.

11. Is Deus auctōritātem patrī dedit.

12. Deus eam auctōritātem matrī dabat.

13. Florem in eā mensā posuit.

14. Eī agricolae in pulchrīs villīs habitant.

15. Pulchrae villae prope eam brevem viam sunt.

H. Give a synopsis of the following verbs.
    1. *videō*—second person, plural

    2. *faciō*—first person, singular

    3. *cupiō*—third person, plural

    4. *incipiō*—second person, singular

    5. *interficiō*—first person, plural

6. *moneō*—third person, singular

I. Answer the following questions.

1. What are the case endings for the Third Declension?

2. What are the case endings for the Fourth Declension?

3. What are the case endings for the Fifth Declension?

4. What is the accusative plural ending for *rēs*?

5. What is the Second Principal Part of *perveniō*?

6. What is the way to say *that* if it points out a masculine noun in the accusative case?

7. What is the way to say *these* if it points out a feminine noun in the dative case?

8. What is the way to say *those* if it points out a neuter noun in the ablataive case?

9. What is the way to say *this* if it points out a masculine noun in the nominative case?

10. What is the way to say *that* if it points out a feminine noun in the accusative case?

DEMONSTRATIVES AS PRONOUNS

A demonstrative pronoun replaces a noun which has been mentioned before. This noun is called the pronoun's antecedent. In Latin, a pronoun agrees with its antecedent in gender and number, but its case is determined by its own use in the sentence. In English and in Latin, a demonstrative pronoun *shows* or *points out* a previously mentioned person or thing.

Because pronouns must be able to replace nouns, they must have the different cases that nouns have, and they must be able to reflect whether they are singular or plural. In addition, each pronoun has to be able to show its gender—whether it is masculine, feminine, or neuter. In our specific case of demonstrative pronouns, the same paradigms are used as for the demonstrative adjective. Instead of modifying a noun, they now replace a noun. Thus, *hic, haec, hoc* still means *this, these,* but it may be replacing *this horse, these guards,* etc. *Ille, illa, illud* still means *that, those,* but it may replace *that horse, those guards* which were mentioned previously. *Is, ea, id* adds a new dimension to its meanings. It still means *this, that / these, those,* but when it is replacing a person it may also mean *he, she, it.*

Let's look at how this use of demonstrative pronouns is helpful in daily conversation. Instead of saying, "*Vīdisne hunc virum?*" (Did you see this man?) and the receiving the response, "*Vīdī hunc virum,*" (I saw this man.); we may simply respond, "*Eum vīdī.*" or, if the emphasis needs to be on a man close by, "*Hunc vīdī.*" The hearers understand the pronoun to be referring to the man about whom the question was asked.

EXERCISE TWENTY-SEVEN

A. Spell out in English how each Latin word should be pronounced and place the accent properly.

1. eōrum

2. eārum

3. eī

4. illud

5. eius

6. eō

7. eōs

8. illōrum

B. Chant each of the following paradigms ten times through.

is, is, ī, em, e! ēs, um, ibus, ēs, ibus!

us, ūs, uī, um, ū! ūs, uum, ibus, ūs, ibus!

ēs, ēī, ēī, em, ē! ēs, ērum, ēbus, ēs, ēbus!

hic, haec, hoc! huius, huius, huius! huic, huic, huic! hunc, hanc, hoc! hōc, hāc, hōc!

hī, hae, haec! hōrum, hārum, hōrum! hīs, hīs, hīs! hōs, hās, haec! hīs, hīs, hīs!

ille, illa, illud! illīus, illīus, illīus! illī, illī, illī! illum, illam, illud! illō, illā, illō!

illī, illae, illa! illōrum, illārum, illōrum! illīs, illīs, illīs! illōs, illās, illa! illīs, illīs, illīs!

is, ea, id! eius, eius, eius! eī, eī, eī! eum, eam, id! eō, eā, eō!

eī, eae, ea! eōrum, eārum, eōrum! eīs, eīs, eīs! eōs, eās, ea! eīs, eīs, eīs!

C. Write the four principal parts of the following verbs. Then chant each verb "set" ten times through.

maneō

capiō

feriō

currō

mittō

respondeō

D. Decline:

is canis

illa lēx

hoc mare

E. Translate the following review sentences.

1. Rēx spem habet.

2. Rem fēminārum audiō.

3. Pater dormīvit.

4. Pater impetum impedīvit.

5. Dormīvimus.

6. Diēs pervenit.

7. Convēnistis.

8. Rēx famam iuvenis audit.

9. Fīlius canem audit.

10. Longam viam invēnistī.

F. Translate the following English into Latin. We will use the same sentences from last lesson, modifiying them to use both the demonstrative pronouns and adjectives.

1. This woman hears the law of God, that one does not hear it.

2. That mother comes upon this road, but she does not walk on it.

3. The woman hinders the arrival of this king and she does not love him.

4. These farmers arrive. Do those arrive?

5. These poets sleep, but those always labor.

6. Those women come and see, but they do not work.

7. They heard this attack, but it was not serious.

8. This king heard that attack and he went to fight.

9. These poets saw that girl, but she did not see them.

10. This woman hindered that man and sent him to the island.

11. This horse is running in the field with him.

12. He overcomes the horse.

13. Did you see those swift birds and did you hear them?

14. Why are they (these tired watchmen) standing in the river?

15. Those men have fought a long war and they have fought it with sharp arrows.

G. Translate the following Latin into English. The words in ( ) are for referral only. Do not translate them.

1. Illum (rēgem) audīvit.

2. Illās (fēminās) audiō.

3. Haec (māter gravis) dormit.

4. Hic (pater) fīlium impedit.

5. Hī (poētae) illās (puellās) spectant.

6. Hic (agricola) dormīvit.

7. Ille (rēx) Deum laudāvit.

8. Illae (fēminae) audient.

9. Māter illōs (servōs) audit.

10. Illam (viam) invēnistis.

11. Is (Deus) auctōritātem patrī dedit.

12. Deus eam (auctōritātem) matrī dabat.

13. Florem in eā (mensā) posuit.

14. Eī (agricolae) in pulchrīs villīs habitant.

15. Eae (Pulchrae villae) prope eam brevem viam sunt.

H. Give a synopsis of the following verbs.

1. *maneō*—second person, plural

2. *capiō*—first person, singular

3. *feriō*—third person, plural

4. *currō*—second person, singular

5. *mittō*—first person, plural

6. *respondeō*—third person, singular

I. Answer the following questions.

    1. What are the case endings for the Third Declension?

    2. What are the case endings for the Fourth Declension?

    3. What are the case endings for the Fifth Declension?

    4. What is the accusative plural ending for *rēs*?

    5. What is the Second Principal Part of *perveniō*?

6. What is the way to say *that* if it refers to a masculine noun in the accusative case?

7. What is the way to say *these* if it refers to a feminine noun in the dative case?

8. What is the way to say *those* if it refers to a neuter noun in the ablataive case?

9. What is the way to say *this* if it refers to a masculine noun in the nominative case?

10. What is the way to say *that* if it refers to a feminine noun in the accusative case?

RELATIVE PRONOUNS

A relative clause is a subordinate clause in a sentence which *relates* or *refers* to a word in another (usually previous) clause. Another name for this type of clause in English is an adjective clause, because the entire clause modifies a noun in another part of the sentence. The relative pronoun *quī, quae, quod* means *who, which.*

For example:

Prometheus was the god who carried fire to earth.

[____main clause____]{____relative clause____}

In this example, *who carried fire to earth* cannot stand by itself as a complete sentence. It is a subordinate or dependent clause. It is a special kind of dependent clause, a *relative clause.* This group of words acts as a modifier of *god.* It tells which god Prometheus was. In this example *who* is the relative pronoun and *god* is the antecedent. A clause which is introduced (begun) by a *relative pronoun* is called a *relative clause.* When we write this sentence in Latin, *who* agrees with *god* in gender (masculine) and number (singular), but it takes its case from its use in the relative clause (nominative because it is the subject).

In Latin the sentence looks like this:

Prōmētheus deus est quī ignem ad terram portāvit.

You will see from the next paradigm that *quī* is masculine, singular, nominative of the relative pronoun.

	MASCULINE	FEMININE	NEUTER
SINGULAR			
NOMINATIVE	quī	quae	quod
GENITIVE	cuius	cuius	cuius
DATIVE	cui	cui	cui
ACCUSATIVE	quem	quam	quod
ABLATIVE	quō	quā	quō
PLURAL			
NOMINATIVE	quī	quae	quae
GENITIVE	quōrum	quārum	quōrum
DATIVE	quīs	quīs	quīs
ACCUSATIVE	quōs	quās	quae
ABLATIVE	quibus	quibus	quibus

When *cum* is used with the relative pronoun to express *ablative of accompaniment, cum* is usually a suffix of the pronoun: *quōcum, quācum, quibuscum.* It means *with whom* or *with which.*

EXERCISE TWENTY-EIGHT

A. Spell out in English how each Latin word should be pronounced and place the accent properly.

1. quī

2. quae

3. quod

4. cuius

5. cui

B. Chant each of the following paradigms ten times through.

is, is, ī, em, e! ēs, um, ibus, ēs, ibus!

us, ūs, uī, um, ū! ūs, uum, ibus, ūs, ibus!

ēs, ēī, ēī, em, ē! ēs, ērum, ēbus, ēs, ēbus!

hic, haec, hoc! huius, huius, huius! huic, huic, huic! hunc, hanc, hoc! hōc, hāc, hōc!

hī, hae, haec! hōrum, hārum, hōrum! hīs, hīs, hīs! hōs, hās, haec! hīs, hīs, hīs!

ille, illa, illud! illīus, illīus, illīus! illī, illī, illī! illum, illam, illud! illō, illā, illō!

illī, illae, illa! illōrum, illārum, illōrum! illīs, illīs, illīs! illōs, illās, illa! illīs, illīs, illīs!

is, ea, id! eius, eius, eius! eī, eī, eī! eum, eam, id! eō, eā, eō!

eī, eae, ea! eōrum, eārum, eōrum! eīs, eīs, eīs! eōs, eās, ea! eīs, eīs, eīs!

quī, quae, quod! cuius, cuius, cuius! cui, cui, cui! quem, quam, quod! quō, quā, quō!

quī, quae, quae! quōrum, quārum, quōrum! quīs, quīs, quīs! quōs, quās, quae! quibus, quibus, quibus!

C. Write the four principal parts of the following verbs. Then chant each verb "set" ten times through.

rogō

maneō

moneō

habeō

dīcō

mittō

D. Decline:

magnus canis

longa lēx

mare quiētum

E. Translate the following review sentences. The words in ( ) are only for reference. Do not translate them.

1. Hic (agricola) dormīvit.

2. Ille (rēx) Deum laudāvit.

3. Illae (fēminae) audient.

4. Māter illōs (servōs) audit.

5. Illam (viam) invēnistis.

6. Is (Deus) auctōritātem patrī dedit.

7. Deus eam (auctōritātem) matrī dabat.

8. Florem in eā (mensā) posuit.

9. Eī (agricolae) in pulchrīs villīs habitant.

10. Eae (Pulchrae villae) prope eam brevem viam sunt.

F. Translate the following English into Latin.

1. This woman who hears the law of God does not love it.

2. That mother who comes upon this road walks on it.

3. The woman who hinders the arrival of this king does not love him.

4. These farmers who are working in the fields arrive.

5. These poets who do not always labor sleep.

6. Those women, whom they watched, did not carry burdens.

7. They heard this attack which was not serious.

8. This king heard the army which he went to fight.

9. These poets saw the girl, who did not see them.

10. The woman who hindered that man sent him to the island.

G. Read the following passage. As you read, follow these five commands:

1) Underline each relative pronoun and circle its antecedent. Draw an arrow to show the relationship.
2) Tell the case and the reason for that case for each relative pronoun.
3) Put an X on all the adjectives which modify feminine nouns.
4) Draw a box around all the verbs in the perfect tense.
5) Double underline the imperative verbs. (They give a command.)

Vir Qui non est Trepidus

Olim rēx Babylōnicus cum Isrāēlītīs pugnāvit, quōs facile vīcit. Deinde ad rēgiam paucōs puerōs Isrāēlītārum captīvōs dūxit, inter quōs erat Daniēl.

Daniēlī, quī propter sapientiam ēgregius erat, rēx dedit multa praemia et multōs honōrēs.

Sociī rēgis autem, quī invidiōsī erant, dīxērunt, "O rēx, Daniēl neque deōs Babylōnicōs neque tē ipsum, rēgem huius terrae, adōrat. Lēge Babylōnicā Daniēl perīre dēbet."

Propter haec verba sociōrum, rēx miserrimus Daniēlem in spēluncam ubi erant multī leōnēs iēcit.

Daniēl autem nōn erat territus; clāmāvit, "Deus quem adōrō mē servābit!"

Rēx dīxit, "Es fīdus, Daniēl; deus tuus, quem semper adōrās, tē servābit."

Postridiē rēx māne ad spēluncam properāvit et magnā vōce Daniēlem vocāvit, "O, Daniēl, servāvitne tē deus quem adōrās?"

Ex spēluncā Daniēl respondit, "O rēx, angelus vēnit, quī apud mē in hāc spēluncā mānsit. Leōnēs mē nōn vulnerāvērunt. Deus mē servāvit!"

Tum rēx populō dīxit, "Studium et scientia et sapientia sunt in hōc virō. Deus quī Daniēlem servāvit deus vērus est. Capite illōs quī eum accūsāvērunt! Illōs iacite in eandem spēluncam ubi leōnēs sunt!"

H. Give a synopsis of the following verbs.

1. *audiō*—second person, plural

2. *inveniō*—first person, singular

3. *veniō*—third person, plural

4. *impediō*—second person, singular

5. *dormiō*—first person, plural

6. *conveniō*—third person, singular

I. Answer the following questions.

1. What are the case endings for the Third Declension?

2. What are the case endings for the Fourth Declension?

3. What are the case endings for the Fifth Declension?

4. What is the accusative plural ending for *manus*?

5. What is the Second Principal Part of *ambulō*?

6. What is the way to say *that* if it modifies a masculine noun in the accusative case?

7. What is the way to say *these* if it refers to a feminine noun in the dative case?

8. What is the way to say *those* if it modifies a neuter noun in the ablataive case?

9. What is the way to say *this* if it refers to a masculine noun in the nominative case?

10. What is the way to say *that* if it modifies a feminine noun in the accusative case?

PASSIVE VOICE

Up to this point we have been able to say many things using the *active voice* of all the verbs. In the active voice, the subject of the sentence is doing the action.

Now we will learn about the *passive* voice of verbs. In a sentence using a *passive* verb, the subject of the sentence is being acted *upon*. This knowledge will give us new ways to express ourselves more precisely.

For instance, the mental picture is quite different if we say, "The boy walks the dog," than if we say, "The boy is walked by the dog."

Or consider this:

The king gives a horse to the man.
Rēx virō equum dat.

The horse is given to the man by the king.
Equus virō ā rēge datur.

The man is given a horse by the king.
Vir equum ā rēge datur.

Each sentence has a different emphasis. In the first sentence our attention is on the king, in the second it is on the horse, in the third it is on the man. In all these sentences, the king is doing the action, thought he is not always the subject. From these examples we see that the active voice makes a very strong statement, but it is quite useful to have the *passive voice* when we want to emphasize the recipient of the action.

ABLATIVE OF PERSONAL AGENT

Notice that in the second and third sentences, the action is done *ā rēge* (by the king). Of course, you recognize this case as the *ablative case*. This use of the ablative, however, is a new one.

To express the person or animal by whom the action of a passive verb is done, use *ā, ab* followed by the ablative case. This use of the ablative is called *ablative of personal agent* and is only used with passive verbs.

FORMING THE PRESENT SYSTEM PASSIVE VOICE

Since you have learned all four conjugations of verbs, the formation of the *passive voice* will follow smoothly. In the present system (present, imperfect, and future tenses) the passive endings are the same for all four conjugations. The passive endings are: *-r, -ris, -tur, -mur, -minī, -ntur.*
To conjugate a verb in

PRESENT TENSE, PASSIVE VOICE: find the present stem and add the passive endings;

IMPERFECT TENSE, PASSIVE VOICE: find the present stem, add the imperfect tense indicator (*bā* or *ēbā*), then add the passive endings;

FUTURE TENSE, PASSIVE VOICE: find the present stem, add the future tense indicator (*bi* or *ē*), then add the passive endings;

PRESENT PASSIVE INDICATIVE

FIRST CONGUGATION

vocor	*I am called*	vocāmur	*we are called*
vocāris	*you are called*	vocāminī	*you are called*
vocātur	*he is called*	vocantur	*they are called*

IMPERFECT PASSIVE INDICATIVE

vocābar	*I was called*	vocābāmur	*we were called*
vocābāris	*you were called*	vocābāminī	*you were called*
vocābātur	*he was called*	vocābantur	*they were called*

FUTURE PASSIVE INDICATIVE

vocābor	*I shall be called*	vocābimur	*we shall be called*
vocāberis	*you will be called*	vocābiminī	*you will be called*
vocābitur	*he will be called*	vocābunter	*they will be called*

PRESENT PASSIVE INDICATIVE

SECOND CONJ.	THIRD CONJ.	THIRD -IO	FOURTH CONJ.
SINGULAR			
videor	regor	capior	audior
vidēris	regeris*	caperis*	audīris
vidētur	regitur	capiar	audiar
PLURAL			
vidēmur	regimur	capimur	audīmur
vidēminī	regiminī	capiminī	audīminī
videntur	reguntur	capiunter	audiuntur

IMPERFECT PASSIVE INDICATIVE

SECOND CONJ.	THIRD CONJ.	THIRD -IO	FOURTH CONJ.
SINGULAR			
vidēbar, etc.	regēbar, etc.	capiēbar, etc.	audiēbar, etc.
PLURAL			
vidēbāmur, etc.	regiēbāmur	capiēbāmur	audiēbāmur

FUTURE PASSIVE INDICATIVE

SECOND CONJ.	THIRD CONJ.	THIRD -IO	FOURTH CONJ.
SINGULAR			
vidēbor, etc.	regar,	capiar	audiar
vidēberis	regēris	capiēris	audiēris
vidēbitur	regētur	capiētur	audiētur
PLURAL			
vidēbimur	regiēmur	capiēmur	audiēmur
vidēbiminī	regiēminī	capiēminī	audiēminī
vidēbuntur	regientur	capientur	audientur

*The third conjugation forms its passive the same as the other conjugations. Note, however, that in the second person, singular of the present tense, the inserted vowel is -*e*, rather than the -*i* of the active voice.

FORMING THE PERFECT SYSTEM PASSIVE VOICE

The perfect system (perfect, pluperfect, and future tenses) forms the passive voice differently from the active voice, but it follows a pattern which is easy to learn. Your diligience in memorizing the four principal parts of your vocabulary verbs will reap great rewards for you in this lesson. The fourth principal part of a verb is called its perfect passive PARTICIPLE. To form the perfect system, passive voice combine the perfect passive participle with the forms of *sum* (perfect tense), *eram* (pluperfect tense), and *erō* (future perfect tense). Because the perfect passive participle is also an adjective form, it agrees with the subject in gender, number, and case (which, of course, will be nominative).

PERFECT PASSIVE INDICATIVE

FIRST CONGUGATION

vocātus, (-a, -um) sum	*I have been called*	vocātī, (-ae, -a) sumus	*we have been called*
vocātus, (-a, -um) es	*you have been called*	vocātī, (-ae, -a) estis	*you have been called*
vocātus, (-a, -um) est	*he has been called*	vocātī, (-ae, -a) sunt	*they have been called*

PLUPERFECT PASSIVE INDICATIVE

vocātus, (-a, -um) eram	*I had been called*	vocātī, (-ae, -a) erāmus	*we had been called*
vocātus, (-a, -um) erās	*you had been called*	vocātī, (-ae, -a) erātis	*you had been called*
vocātus, (-a, -um) erat	*he had been called*	vocātī, (-ae, -a) erant	*they had been called*

FUTURE PASSIVE INDICATIVE

vocātus, (-a, -um) erō	*I shall have been called*	vocātī, (-ae, -a) erimus	*we have been called*
vocātus, (-a, -um) eris	*you will have been called*	vocātī, (-ae, -a) eritis	*you have been called*
vocātus, (-a, -um) erit	*he will have been called*	vocātī, (-ae, -a) erunt	*they have been called*

PERFECT PASSIVE INDICATIVE

	SECOND CONJ.	THIRD CONJ.	THIRD -IO	FOURTH CONJ.
SINGULAR	vīsus, (-a, -um) sum	rēctus, (-a, -um) sum	captus, (-a, -um) sum	audītus, (-a, -um) sum
PLURAL	vīsī, (-ae, -a) sumus	rēctī, (-ae, -a) sumus	captī, (-ae, -a) sumus	audītī, (-ae, -a) sumus

PLUPERFECT PASSIVE INDICATIVE

	SECOND CONJ.	THIRD CONJ.	THIRD -IO	FOURTH CONJ.
SINGULAR	vīsus, (-a, -um) eram	rēctus, (-a, -um) eram	captus, (-a, -um) eram	audītus, (-a, -um) eram
PLURAL	vīsī, (-ae, -a) erāmus	rēctī, (-ae, -a) erāmus	captī, (-ae, -a) erāmus	audītī, (-ae, -a) erāmus

FUTURE PASSIVE INDICATIVE

	SECOND CONJ.	THIRD CONJ.	THIRD -IO	FOURTH CONJ.
SINGULAR	vīsus, (-a, -um) erō	rēctus, (-a, -um) erō	captus, (-a, -um) erō	audītus, (-a, -um) erō
PLURAL	vīsī, (-ae, -a) erimus	rēctī, (-ae, -a) erimus	captī, (-ae, -a) erimus	audītī, (-ae, -a) erimus

Exercise Twenty-Nine

A. Spell out in English how each Latin word should be pronounced and place the accent properly. Then translate each form.

1. portor
2. vocābāris
3. vidēbitur
4. capientur
5. audīminī

B. Chant each of the following paradigms ten times through.

is, is, ī, em, e! ēs, um, ibus, ēs, ibus!
us, ūs, uī, um, ū! ūs, uum, ibus, ūs, ibus!
ēs, ēī, ēī, em, ē! ēs, ērum, ēbus, ēs, ēbus!
hic, haec, hoc! huius, huius, huius! huic, huic, huic! hunc, hanc, hoc! hōc, hāc, hōc!
hī, hae, haec! hōrum, hārum, hōrum! hīs, hīs, hīs! hōs, hās, haec! hīs, hīs, hīs!
ille, illa, illud! illīus, illīus, illīus! illī, illī, illī! illum, illam, illud! illō, illā, illō!
illī, illae, illa! illōrum, illārum, illōrum! illīs, illīs, illīs! illōs, illās, illa! illīs, illīs, illīs!
is, ea, id! eius, eius, eius! eī, eī, eī! eum, eam, id! eō, eā, eō!
eī, eae, ea! eōrum, eārum, eōrum! eīs, eīs, eīs! eōs, eās, ea! eīs, eīs, eīs!
quī, quae, quod! cuius, cuius, cuius! cui, cui, cui! quem, quam, quod! quō, quā, quō!
quī, quae, quae! quōrum, quārum, quōrum! quīs, quīs, quīs! quōs, quās, quae! quibus, quibus, quibus!
r, ris, tur! mur, minī, ntur!

C. Write the four principal parts of the following verbs. Then chant each verb "set" ten times through.

cupiō
faciō
feriō
dūcō
veniō

D. Decline:

bōs novus

arbor ūmida

carmen gratum

Challenge:

cursus celeris

rēs facilis

E. Translate the following English into Latin.

1. I was carried from the building.

2. You were seen by God.

3. He will be held by the fierce youth.

4. We haven't been frightened by the tired lions.

5. You (pl.) had been filled with good food.

6. They will have been recognized near the water.

7. I have been guided to this place.

8. She had been left behind to work in the house (domus).

9. He will have been accepted.

10. You had been wished a good journey.

F. Read the following passage. Give a verbatim (word by word) translation of each sentence which contains a passive verb.

ARIES AUREUS

Olim in terrā longinquā habitābant frāter et soror, Phrixus et Hellē. [1]Hī līberī autem crūdēliter (*cruelly*) vexābantur. Dī Olympī igitur frātrem sorōremque servāre (*to save*) cupiēbant.

Mercurius in conciliō deōrum dīxit, "Hōs līberōs ex patriā ad locum tūtum portābō, sed iter perīculōsum erit."

[2]Frāter sororque in magnō agrō ubi ovēs erant saepe vidēbantur. [3]Ab ovēs nōn vulnerābantur.

[4]Olim, autem (*however*), ariēs (*ram*) aureus inter ovēs vīsus est ā līberīs. Is ariēs nōn erat ferus. [5]Rē vērā (*in truth*) quiētus erat, dum (*while* (with pres. tense) corōnīs (*garlands, crowns*) adōrnātur. Tum frāter et soror in tergum (-ī, *N. back*) arietis ascendērunt (*climbed*). [6]Subitō ariēs volāre (*to fly*) incēpit, et līberī territī in caelum celeriter (*quickly*), portābantur.

[7]Ab ariete trāns montēs, flūmina, maria volātī sunt. Tum Hellē dēfessa dē tergō arietis in mare angustum (*narrow*) cecidit (*fell*). Phrixus tristis (*sad*) erat.

Post multās horās ariēs Phrixum tūtum (*safely*) dēposuit in Colchide, terrā cuius rēx benignus (*kind*) erat.

[8]Ibi (*there*) vōx ā Phrixō audītus est, "Sacrificā hunc arietem, sed servā vellus (-eris, N. *fleece*). Pōne vellus in arbore sacrā. [9]Sum Mercurius; dracō (*dragon*) mittētur quī noctū et interdiū arborem spectābit." Posteā Phrixus vellus ad rēgiam (*palace*) portāvit. Rēx, ubi fābulam arietis aureī audīvit, dīxit, "Tū (*you*)eris fīlius meus. [10]Vellus aureum saepe quaerētur (quaerō- *to seek, to search for*). Magnus honor ad rēgnum meum veniet."

G. Give a synopsis of the following verbs *in the passive voice.*

1. *mutō*—second person, plural

2. *habeō*—first person, singular

3. *veniō*—third person, plural

4. *impediō*—second person, singular

5. *dīcō*—first person, plural

6. *conveniō*—third person, singular

H. Answer the following questions.

   1. What are the present system, passive voice, verb endings?

   2. What are the case endings for the First Declension?

   3. What are the case endings for the Second Declension?

   4. What is the accusative plural ending for *ovis*?

   5. What is the Second Principal Part of *impediō*?

   6. How many conjugations are there?

   7. How many declensions are there?

   8. What is apposition?

   9. What is a predicate nominative?

   10. What case does the preposition *ad* take?

NOTES